# DESIGN YOUR OWN TEES

DISCARDED

# DESIGN YOUR OWN TEES

## Techniques and Inspiration
to Stitch, Stamp, Stencil, and
Silk-Screen Your Very Own T-shirts

JENNIFER COOKE

ST. MARTIN'S GRIFFIN
NEW YORK

DESIGN YOUR OWN TEES

Copyright © 2010 by Quirk Packaging, Inc.

Photography copyright © 2010 by Jennifer Cooke

All rights reserved.

Printed in Singapore.

For information, address St. Martin's Press, 175 Fifth Avenue, New York, NY 10010.

www.stmartins.com

A Quirk Packaging Book

Design by woolypear

Editing by Erin Canning and Erin Slonaker

Illustrations by Jennifer Cooke

Library of Congress Cataloging-in-Publication Data Available Upon Request

ISBN: 978-0-312-64424-6

First Edition: October 2010

10  9  8  7  6  5  4  3  2  1

To my parents, James and Janet Cooke,
for their endless support of my creativity.

## ACKNOWLEDGMENTS

This book came about through a chance meeting with BJ Berti at St. Martin's Press. Thanks, BJ, for giving me the opportunity to write it! And thanks to everyone at St. Martin's, especially Jasmine Faustino. To the folks at Quirk Packaging—Sharyn Rosart, Lynne Yeamans, and Erin Canning—thank you for your patience, guidance, and unfailing good humor. Also thanks to my agent, Kate McKean, for the advice and encouragement. To Lana Lê at woolypear, thanks for turning all of this into something very lovely.

Many fabulous friends agreed to model for me: Cherish Cullison, Gabriele Donati, Zoe Giles, Becky Haliscelik, Nim Lee, and Michelle Santangelo—thanks for your amazing generosity, and for bringing these T-shirts to life! A special thanks to Becky, for the expert Photoshop help.

I could not have written this book or done the work leading up to it without the love and support of my family and friends. Thank you especially to Molly, for your insight and vision, and Joanna, for the sisterly love and the long hours spent debriefing the creative life. And to my ever-so-patient husband, Sean, who lived through all of the joys and challenges of this book with me, helped with opinions, pictures and projects, and even married me between book deadlines. Thank you.

# Contents

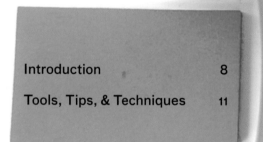

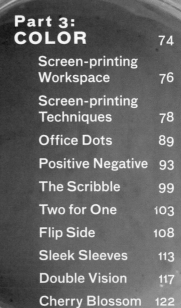

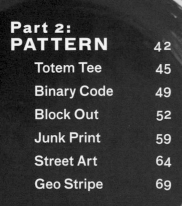

# Introduction

These days, there is a renewed appreciation for handmade arts and crafts because of their personal touch. I've been making and selling tees for more than a decade, and I've written *Design Your Own Tees* to show you how easily you can bring an artisanal quality into your wardrobe by embellishing T-shirts with your own designs.

T-shirts are classic; everyone wears them—and decorating your own tees gives you the opportunity to express your artistic vision or share your crafty enthusiasms. My goal is to inspire you to turn your tees into bold, graphic, personal statements, which is especially meaningful in this era of mass production.

The T-shirt design projects presented here are divided into three parts: Texture, Pattern, and Color. These loose concept groupings present various techniques—all easy to master—for T-shirt embellishment, while inviting you to consider creative ways to use texture, pattern, and color in your designs.

Mix and match projects for increased depth and layers. Add, subtract, and create your way to a bright, personalized T-shirt wardrobe. You'll have fun and come up with some great new tees in the meantime. Long live handmade!

—JENNIFER COOKE

# GETTING STARTED

T-shirt design is a creative endeavor. Like any artistic process, there are many twists and turns along the road between starting and finishing a project. Here are a couple of golden rules to keep the whole experience fun and rewarding.

## Test everything first.

The most important thing I've learned in ten years of making tees is that things never go exactly how you think they will, especially when you're trying new techniques. While I've given you the instructions and designs to successfully create all of the projects in this book, you should be sure to practice on scrap fabrics before you get ready to print or sew your final product. This will save you a lot of headaches.

## Love your mistakes.

Printing often goes awry. I can't tell you how many times I've discovered that an "accident" is a lot more interesting than what I'd planned. Maybe you can salvage an imperfect print by printing another image on top. And of course, the beauty of a handmade tee lies in its imperfections.

## Wear appropriate clothing.

This may seem obvious, but fabric paints and inks are made to adhere to clothing permanently. I've found that it is nearly impossible to completely remove inks and paints, even if they haven't been heat-set, so plan carefully.

# Tools, Tips, & Techniques

## FABRIC

### T-shirt Types

For certain projects in this book, I suggest that particular knits of tees be used for good results. Embroidering on a rib-knit tee, for example, will be more difficult than embroidering on a flat-knit one; for printing projects, a flat-knit tee will give you the best results. But do experiment—you may decide you love the unexpected look of your artwork on a very chunky knit like the rib of a sweatshirt.

### Material Types

I recommend using cotton or cotton blends for printing projects. Most paints or inks may not adhere well to synthetics. You can check with the manufacturer of the fabric paints you are using for specifics; if you want to try printing on a fabric they don't recommend, do a test first to see if it works. You must heat-set and wash the fabric to complete the test and make sure you get good results. The print itself will probably look great on whatever fabric you use—it's the washability of the inks that is the question here.

## Fabric Preparation

Manufacturers always recommend that fabrics be washed before printing. This is to remove any sizing that may interfere with the ability of the ink to adhere to the fabric.

## Heat-setting

Fabric paints and inks need to be heat-set after they have been printed. Heat-setting makes images washfast. Finished garments can be ironed on the reverse side for several minutes or dried in a commercial dryer for twenty to thirty minutes to set the ink. Use the hottest dryer setting available—the prints you've made should be hot to the touch when you remove the garment from the dryer. (Home dryers do not get hot enough to do this; take your tees to the laundromat to dry them.) Some inks come with an additive that can be mixed in with the ink to make them washfast and eliminate the need for heat-setting. Check the manufacturer's directions on the paints or inks you are using for specific heat-setting requirements.

**TIP**

Always do a test when using new materials. You want these projects to last, and there is nothing more disappointing than taking your new T-shirt out of the wash to see that the image has disappeared because it wasn't heat-set properly. If you have difficulty with a certain brand or product, try a different one.

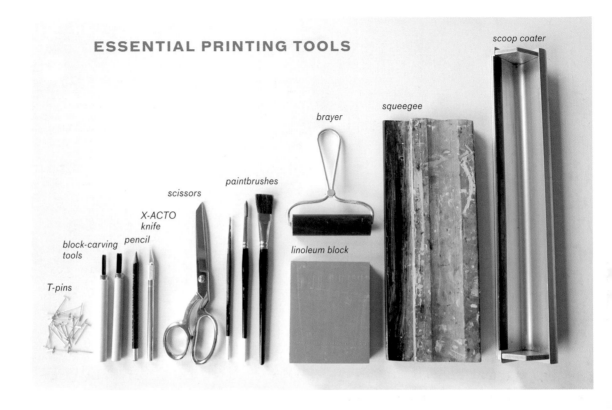

**ESSENTIAL PRINTING TOOLS**

scoop coater

squeegee

brayer

paintbrushes

scissors

X-ACTO knife

pencil

block-carving tools

linoleum block

T-pins

# PAINTS AND INKS FOR FABRIC

There are many different fabric paints and inks available to use in your projects. Most of these are transparent, meaning they will allow the color on which they are printed to show through. Others are opaque; these will cover the color they are printed on. Consider this when you are deciding which materials to use for your project. That yellow transparent ink may look fabulous in the container, but if you print it on a black T-shirt, it is going to disappear. *Note: Unless I've instructed otherwise, I recommend using water-based paints and inks for all of your projects. Many professional screen-printing inks are not water-based and will never dry without proper equipment, so keep this in mind when purchasing screen-printing supplies.*

## OVERLAPPING TRANSPARENT COLORS

color 1                                                                        color 2

*(overlapping result)*

## Transparent Ink

If you are printing on light-colored fabrics, transparent
inks are great. You can use transparency to your advantage—
if you print one color of ink on top of another, you can
create a third color in your design.

## Opaque Ink

Opaque inks usually come in a more limited color palette,
but they can be mixed with transparent inks to create a wide
variety of colors. I often mix opaque white with different
colors to create light shades that I can print on dark
fabrics. There are also opaque metallic colors available,
which can add a luxe feel to projects.

# CREATING YOUR OWN ARTWORK FOR PRINTING

For all of the printing projects described in this book, you have the option of using the provided artwork (see Templates, page 126) or creating your own. If you create your own artwork, you will need to make a different image for each color you want to print. These color-specific images are called color separations; each image will be applied to its own printing block, stencil, or silk screen, depending on the technique you are using. The images will then be applied to your tee, one at a time.

In the illustrations below, I want to create a T-shirt with a graphic of birds in one color and flowers in another color. I first draw my bird art and flower art separately, then apply them to their own printing blocks or stencils in order to create the final tee.

## CREATING YOUR OWN ARTWORK EXAMPLE

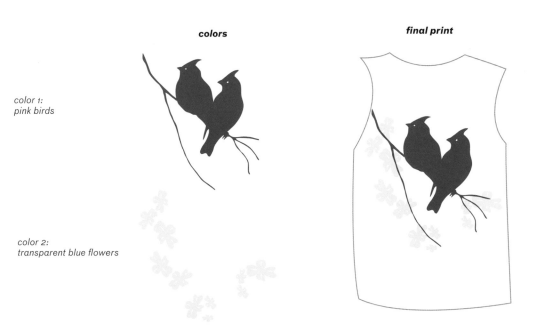

*colors*

*final print*

*color 1:*
*pink birds*

*color 2:*
*transparent blue flowers*

# part 1

TEXTURE

For your first T-shirts, I invite you to try some simple projects that play with texture— a wonderful and often forgotten direction for T-shirt embellishment.

These projects will get you thinking about T-shirt design in a new way. You'll use fabrics, ribbons, stitches, and photos to create visual interest, depth, and varied surfaces. Using bold geometric shapes, you'll move beyond the usual T-shirt graphics to come up with edgy and elegant designs.

**TECHNIQUE: Machine Stitching**

# MACHINE

This project was inspired by the fabric covered in test stitches I got back from the repair shop when I took my sewing machine in for servicing. I found the decorative stitches to be beautiful and complex. Since I have never used most of these stitches on my machine, I experimented with layering them to create a tangled wave of lines. The stitches create beautiful, unexpected textures on the knit fabric of a T-shirt. Explore your sewing machine's potential by creating your own linear patterns!

## Machine Wave

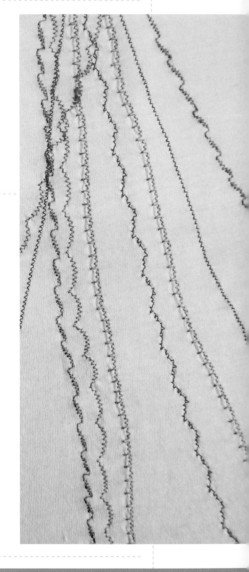

### WHAT YOU'LL NEED

[ ] Test fabric

[ ] T-shirt

[ ] Thread in a variety of colors

[ ] Sewing machine with decorative stitch options

[ ] Tailor's chalk (optional)

### HOW TO DO IT

1. Before sewing on your T-shirt, use the test fabric to try out the different decorative stitches your machine has to offer. Play with the stitch length and width to see what makes each stitch look interesting. Experiment with colors to find a combination that works well with the color of your tee.

2. Make a design (think number of lines and type of stitches), and decide where you want the lines to go on your shirt. You can keep it simple with just a few lines, or use lots of layers like I've shown here.

3. Start sewing. Remember to backstitch a tiny bit at the beginning and the end of each seam so your threads won't pull out later.

4. Cut off the thread tails (or leave them hanging, if you like), and go!

### TIP

The tee will get bunched up when you put it through the machine, making it difficult to see where you're stitching. You may find it helpful to mark some lines with tailor's chalk that you can follow while you're sewing.

### VARIATION

Try minimizing color, and emphasizing pure texture, with this project. For the stitching, choose a thread that is just a shade lighter or darker than the color of your tee. Your tonal stitch wave will be subtle and lovely.

# HEIRLOOM STAR

## Heirloom Star

Many T-shirt design projects require some kind of equipment or are a little messy. To counterbalance those studio intensives, I always like to have a good, portable, low-tech project that can be worked on anywhere. For tees, embroidery is it! Hand stitching takes time, but it is well worth it for the texture, detail, and heirloom quality. Here, I've created a star pattern using a simple straight stitch. Follow this pattern or come up with your own to create a sweet tee that you'll want to wear forever.

## WHAT YOU'LL NEED

[ ] Flat-knit T-shirt (It is difficult to keep your stitches uniform on a rib-knit tee.)

[ ] Embroidery floss in a selection of colors

[ ] Stabilizer

[ ] Embroidery hoop (I prefer plastic to wood, as it doesn't snag on the fabric.)

[ ] Tapestry needle

[ ] Tracing paper (optional)

## HOW TO DO IT

1. Enlarge or minimize the star pattern provided (page 126) to the desired size, or come up with your own design. If you would like to use tracing paper as a guide for your stitches, trace the star pattern onto the tracing paper. Don't worry about colors—the tracing paper serves as a stitching guide only. (Personally, I prefer to stitch without it, referring to my pattern as I'm working. But you may find that it keeps your design from getting all wonky while you're stitching.)

2. Cut a piece of stabilizer that is a little larger than the pattern, and pin it to the back of the T-shirt underneath where you plan to stitch.

3. Place the embroidery hoop around the tee where you want the design to appear. You want the fabric to be flat, but don't stretch it; if you pull the fabric too tightly, it will look funny when you are finished.

4. If you are using a tracing-paper pattern, position it over the tee as desired. Now you are ready to start stitching.

5. Start stitching at the center of the star pattern and work out toward the edges, sewing right through the tracing paper and stabilizer. The tracing paper will break apart as you are working, but it will still serve its purpose. Since you will be washing and wearing this garment, you will have to make knots on your cut threads to keep them secure.

6. When you are finished embroidering, you can pull away any of the remaining tracing paper and remove your tee from the embroidery hoop.

7. Cut away any remaining edges of stabilizer.

### TIP

Stabilizer or no stabilizer? There are different kinds of embroidery stabilizer out there. Stabilizer helps to keep your stitching flat when you are working on a knit fabric that stretches. There's a kind that tears away when you are done, a kind that dissolves in water, and a kind that stays there permanently. Or you could just skip it. Experiment to see what works best for you.

### VARIATION

Keep on embroidering, adding more stitches beyond the provided pattern. In the same manner, repeat each circle again, adding more stitches as your star gets bigger. Cover as much of the tee as you can, and your sweet star will turn into something truly galactic!

# ROUGH EDGES

Appliqué is a lovely technique for embellishment. Usually, you finish the edges of your stitched-on designs to keep them neat and protected from damage during washing and wearing. For this project, however, leave the edges raw and let chance take its course! Create a stylish T-shirt dress that is refined enough to wear out on the town. Appliqué different types of fabrics for a varied effect—this is a great project for leftover scraps that are too small to use for anything else. Fabrics will fray at different rates, and some may eventually disappear in the wash, leaving the stitching exposed. Embrace the unpredictable results of this project, and you will have a truly one-of-a-kind tee.

## WHAT YOU'LL NEED

[ ]  T-shirt dress

[ ]  Fabric scraps in a variety of colors and patterns

[ ]  Contrasting thread

[ ]  Scissors or a rotary cutter and cutting mat

[ ]  Straight pins

[ ]  Sewing machine

[ ]  Washing machine

## HOW TO DO IT

1. Make a pattern piece out of the hexagon template provided (page 127), or create your own pattern piece in the shape of your choice. Use paper or lightweight cardboard to do this. Adjust the scale of the hexagon template, if you like.

2. Cut out lots of hexagons from the fabric scraps. You can use scissors or a rotary cutter and cutting mat. *Note: Remember to always roll the rotary cutter away from you—it is very sharp and can give you a nasty cut. (I'm speaking from experience here!)*

3. Arrange the hexagons on your tee in a pattern that pleases you.

4. Pin them in place.

5. Stitch around the edges of the hexagons with a straight stitch. (I chose to stitch my whole project in one contrasting thread color to add some punch.) Remember to leave enough fabric around the edges to allow for some nice fraying.

6. Backstitch to secure each piece.

7. Now it's all up to chance. Wear your tee, and delight in how much it changes each time you wash it.

### TIP

For an extra-personal touch, use some of the printing techniques in this book to print your own fabrics for your appliqués.

### VARIATION

Raw-edged stripes! Cut lengths of fabric about ¾" (2 cm) wide and arrange them on your tee. Stitch each stripe with one seam in the center of the fabric, leaving lots of opportunity for fraying.

# SHINE ON

I love shine, and there's nothing I like better than shiny ribbons. I've used them to create a luxe handbag out of a simple canvas tote. Find ribbons in a variety of colors and textures to make your striped gradient.

I know, this isn't a T-shirt, but you need something great to carry, don't you? And you can use this technique on tees, too, for a shiny trim. Ribbons can get wavy when you stitch them directly to the knit fabric of a T-shirt, so I recommend stitching the ribbons to a lightweight, woven fabric first, then stitching the entire piece to your tee. Remember that ribbons won't stretch like the knit of a tee, so you might not want to cover the whole shirt. An accent of a few stripes on the sleeves or hem would be lovely!

## WHAT YOU'LL NEED

[ ] Canvas tote bag
[ ] Ribbons of different colors and sizes. *Note: Avoid very narrow ribbons 1/8" (3 mm) and under. They will get lost in the stitching.*

[ ] Contrasting thread
[ ] Scissors
[ ] Seam ripper
[ ] Sewing machine

## HOW TO DO IT

1. Lay out the ribbons in a pattern that is pleasing to you. Create a loose gradient as I have done here, or arrange them in a random pattern. Use thick and thin widths for a varied effect. Try different textures and patterns.

2. When you have decided on a stripe pattern, cut the ribbons slightly longer than the width of the bag.

3. Rip the side seams of the tote with a seam ripper, so you can lay the bag out flat, like a long rectangle, with the handles on the short ends.

4. Select the zigzag stitch on your sewing machine. Play with the stitch width and length until you find a look that you like. The stitch should be wide enough to cover the edges of two pieces of ribbon placed next to each other.

5. Add a ribbon or some decorative stitching to the handles. By doing this before you start sewing the ribbons on the main part of the tote, you will be able to hide the edges of the handle seams under the ribbons.

6. Starting at one end of the tote, stitch one edge of the first ribbon to the bag using the zigzag stitch. Make sure you stitch the ribbons all the way to the edges of the tote—the ribbon edges will get folded over in the seam allowance when you stitch the tote back together.

## TIP

If you're feeling adventurous, you can even jump forward to some of the printing projects starting on page 42, and decorate plain ribbons with your own patterns. That will make this touchable project extra special.

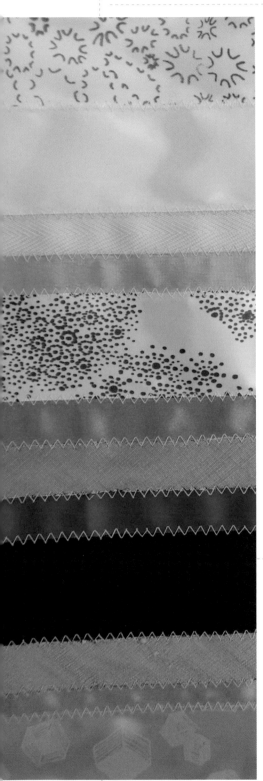

7. Place the second ribbon next to the first one, so that the unstitched edge of the first one touches the edge of the second.

8. Stitch the ribbons to the tote with the zigzag stitch. You should be able to keep the ribbons close together as you are stitching, so that you get a nice flat seam and you won't see any of the tote bag between the two ribbons.

9. Continue stitching until you have covered both sides of the tote with the ribbons.

10. Clip away long ribbon edges along the tote edges, and sew up the sides of the tote.

11. I recommend finishing the seams on the inside so they don't fray. You can use a serger if you have one. If you don't have a serger, create a French seam.

    a. Sew the side seams of the tote with the right sides facing out, so the ribbon stripes are facing outward.

    b. Turn the tote inside out and press the bag flat.

    c. Sew the side seams again, this time stitching ¼" to ½" (5 mm–1.25 cm) toward the center of the bag, or wide enough that the raw edges from your first seams will be covered by your second seams.

12. Turn your bag right-side out, and you're ready to go!

## VARIATION

No need to stop at just ribbons; there are lots of great trims that would make lovely stripes for a tote or a tee. Raid the rickrack section, or cover your project with cute little pom-poms. Stick with one theme for a cohesive graphic look by picking trims that are all variations on the same color. Doing this will keep your project looking sharp and graphic, instead of like the remnants bin at the fabric store.

# FOUND ART

**Found Art**

I enjoy collecting visual inspiration. I have been
saving scraps of paper, photos, and other small items
for a while now, and I have assembled them into a
big collage on my fridge. For this project, I wanted
to transfer some of these images directly onto a
T-shirt and keep the collage-y feel of the original
collection. I scanned the scraps onto the computer
and used iron-on transfer paper to apply them to a
tee. There is a general blue theme to my collection
of papers, which helps them hold together visually.
I threw a couple of pictures from my Diana camera
into the mix. Create your own wearable found-art
collage with things that inspire you.

## WHAT YOU'LL NEED

[ ] Collection of inspiration such as
photos, paper scraps, fabric scraps,
or whatever you like

[ ] Computer with image manipulation
software such as Adobe Photoshop

[ ] Scanner

[ ] Light-colored T-shirt (I used a burnout
tee for added dimension.)

[ ] Iron-on transfer paper for
light-colored fabrics

[ ] Printer

[ ] Scissors

[ ] Pillowcase or lightweight fabric

[ ] Iron

[ ] Hard surface for ironing

## HOW TO DO IT

1. Scan images onto the computer. Ideally, images should be 300 dpi (dots per inch) at the size you want them to print in order to transfer well.

2. All images can use a little help when they are scanned onto the computer. In Adobe Photoshop, I use Levels and Curves to brighten images and make overall color adjustments. You can find these settings in Image > Adjustments. Play with the image to find something you like.

3. Start a new Photoshop file by selecting File > New. In the pop-up dialog box, make the image resolution 300 pixels/inch and no larger than 8" x 10" (20 x 25 cm), the size of the transfer paper.

4. Copy images from your original scans using Select > All, then Edit > Copy.

5. Paste images into your new file with Edit > Paste. Photoshop will automatically paste each image onto a separate layer.

6. Using Photoshop, arrange the images in a pleasing layout. Use the Lasso tool to select images, then use the Move tool to place them where you want them. Keep the Layers palette visible by selecting Window > Layers. (A check mark will show up next to all visible layers.) Highlight the layer you want to modify by clicking on it in the Layers palette. *Note: If you are new to Photoshop, it can be easy to forget to select the appropriate layer for the item you want to move. If you're having trouble selecting and moving images, you are probably working on the wrong layer. You can arrange the order of the layers by dragging and dropping them to where you want them in the Layers palette. Think of this as you would think of a stack of papers—the ones on top will cover the ones underneath.*

## TIP

You are limited by the size of the T-shirt transfer paper, so if you want to make a collage that is bigger than 8" x 10" (20 x 25 cm), you can split up your printout between two or more sheets of paper. It may be difficult to line up two transfers exactly on your tee, but if you keep space in between some of your images as I have here, you won't have to worry about placing things exactly.

7. Your images will transfer in reverse, so after you have completed your layout, make sure that you flip images in the computer. In Photoshop, use Image > Image Rotation > Flip Canvas Horizontal to flip your images.

8. Following the manufacturer's directions, print the T-shirt transfers with your printer.

9. Cut out the transfers as close as you can to the edges of the image. Any blank transfer paper will show up looking clear on your T-shirt.

10. Place the pillowcase or lightweight fabric on the tabletop or hard surface you will be ironing on. Press the fabric and the T-shirt with a dry iron. (You do not want to use an ironing board as the surface is too soft; you do not want to use any steam, either.)

11. With the ironed T-shirt laid out on the fabric and table, arrange your transfer images face down on your tee.

12. Iron the transfers, pressing very hard and moving the iron slowly across the transfers. Follow the manufacturer's directions, ironing for the amount of time specified.

13. Place your tee aside, and let it cool for a few minutes.

14. When it is cool to the touch, peel off the backing of the transfer paper, letting the images from your collage shine through.

## VARIATION

This graphic already has a scrapbook feel—take the concept one step further and make something extra personal. Use old family photos or meaningful memorabilia to commemorate a special event in a clean, graphic style.

# PIXEL PRINT

Photos make great graphics, but sometimes you want to be a little abstract. For this project, I took a favorite photo of alpine flowers and made it geometric by exaggerating the scale of the pixels. Start with a digital photo or scan one onto the computer to create your own pixelated painting.

*My source photo for this project. Look closely to see the final artwork.*

## WHAT YOU'LL NEED

[ ] Digital photo or another scanned image

[ ] Computer with image manipulation software such as Adobe Photoshop

[ ] Light-colored T-shirt

[ ] Iron-on transfer paper for light-colored fabrics

[ ] Printer

[ ] Scissors

[ ] Pillowcase or lightweight fabric

[ ] Iron

[ ] Hard surface for ironing

## Pixel Print

### HOW TO DO IT

1. Scan your image onto the computer, if necessary. You do not need to worry about dpi for this project because you will be reducing the pixel size for dramatic effect.

2. Using Photoshop, scale the image to the size you want it to print. It is important to scale the image first, so that you will get an accurate reading of the pixel size when you adjust it. You can do this in Image > Image Size, and enter the desired height and width of the artwork.

3. Now it is time to get creative. Play with the number of pixels in the image, leaving the dimensions the same. The lower the number, the larger the pixels will be. Use Image > Image Size to do this. Enter a number in the box titled Resolution. Try something, click OK, and look at your image. You will have to zoom in on your image to see what it will look like at the print size. Use View > Zoom In to look more closely at the image. The rulers on the left and top edges of your image will help you with scale. (If you can't see the rulers, use View > Rulers to turn them on.) If you change your mind and want to try a different pixel size, use Edit > Undo Image Size to return to the original image and try again. For my T-shirt, I used two pixels per inch.

4. Once you have decided on the number of pixels, play with the colors. I used Image > Adjustment > Brightness/Contrast to adjust my image. If you wish, play with some of the other Image Adjustment features to tweak your image.

5. When you have the image looking great on screen, you'll need to take another step in Photoshop to make sure it prints correctly. Resize the image one last time; go to Image > Image Size, and reset the Resolution to 300 dpi. At the bottom of the Image Size window, set Resample Image to Nearest Neighbor, and click OK. This last bit is really important—it will keep your image a composition of hard-edged squares.

### TIP

T-shirt transfers are great for quick projects and those times when you want to use photographic images in your work. They aren't the longest-lasting technique in this book, though. If you make a transfer graphic that you want to last a little longer, try taking the image to a local copy shop and having them print and apply the transfer for you with professional heat-transfer equipment.

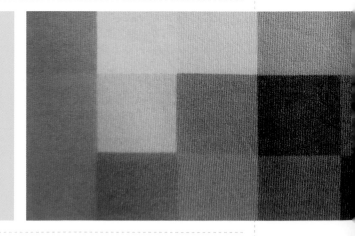

6. The image will transfer in reverse, so after you have completed your layout, make sure that you flip it. In Photoshop, use Image > Image Rotation > Flip Canvas Horizontal to flip your images.

7. Following the manufacturer's directions, print the T-shirt transfers on your printer.

8. Cut out the transfers as close as you can to the edges of the image. Any blank transfer paper will show up looking clear on your T-shirt.

9. Place the pillowcase or lightweight fabric on the tabletop or hard surface you will be ironing on. Press the fabric and the T-shirt with a dry iron. (You do not want to use an ironing board as the surface is too soft; you do not want to use any steam, either.)

10. With the ironed T-shirt laid out on the fabric and table, arrange your transfer image face down on your tee.

11. Iron the transfer, pressing very hard and moving the iron slowly across the transfers. Follow the manufacturer's directions, ironing for the amount of time specified.

12. Place your tee aside, and let it cool for a few minutes. Then remove the backing paper from the transfer. Pixel love!

## VARIATION

I went for an all-out grid effect with my pixel image, but there are so many possibilities to create an abstract image from a photograph. Try adjusting the number of pixels to ten or fifteen per inch. Your image will still look photographic, but it will be abstract and grid-like as well.

# part 2

# Pattern

You're ready to start printing your T-shirts. Fun, right? In this part, we'll explore some basic techniques that give a great handmade feel. Stamping, block printing, and stenciling—all are great ways to begin using your own artwork to decorate tees. And we'll start to look more closely at pattern: the use of repeating elements in a design. These projects use pattern loosely, sometimes repeating a motif just a few times to create a sense of rhythm, and sometimes covering the entire shirt. Try an intuitive approach. With these tees, I didn't worry too much about creating exact repeats—I like the handwrought feel of patterns that are a little bit off.

Take a look around you and you'll see that patterns abound, and lots of those patterns can be great inspiration for your T-shirt projects.

**TECHNIQUE: Potato Stamping**

# Totem Tee

The humble potato. It's cheap, readily available, and fun to use as a stamp for printing. Maybe, like me, you first tried potato printing as a kid. This time, I turned this no-frills technique into something elegant by tracing along the spine of my tee with a scarab image inspired by the art of ancient Egypt. Potato stamps carve up quickly, which makes this a great project for experimentation.

## Totem Tee

## WHAT YOU'LL NEED

[ ] T-shirt

[ ] Potatoes large enough in diameter to accommodate your artwork

[ ] Pencil

[ ] X-ACTO knife

[ ] Fabric paint

[ ] Paintbrush

[ ] Extra fabric or newsprint for testing and padding

## HOW TO DO IT

**1.** Enlarge or minimize the artwork provided (page 127) to the desired size, or create your own image.

**2.** Wash potatoes and cut in half.

**3.** Transfer the images to the potatoes. I do this by drawing directly on the potato with a sharp pencil. The color from the lead won't be visible in the flesh of the potato, but you will be able to make a light carved outline of the image with the pencil.

**4.** Carefully carve out your image with the X-ACTO knife. (This is a reductive printing process, which means you are carving away what you don't want to print, leaving a raised image.) Cut down at least ¼" (5 mm) into the potato. The deeper you cut, the easier it will be to get a good print. Check the printing surface of the image on the potato. Any texture you see will show up when you go to print, so carefully smooth out the surface by carving more potato away with the X-ACTO knife.

*step 4* **CARVING A POTATO**

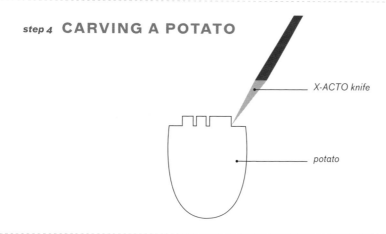

X-ACTO knife

potato

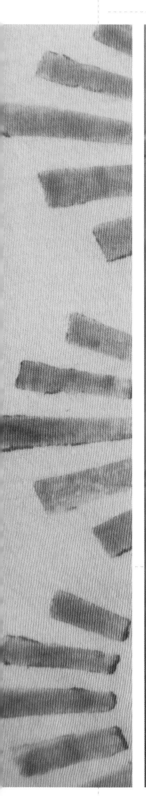

5. When you are finished carving, you are ready to print. I like to use a paintbrush to apply the fabric paint to the potato—it gives me lots of control and allows me to clean up any paint drips with the brush. You can also pour out some paint into a dish and dip the potato in the paint to ink it. (I prefer to use one color of ink per potato.)

6. Do some test prints on a piece of extra fabric to get a feel for your potato stamp and to see what it looks like. If you want to make any adjustments in your design, wash the potato and re-carve it.

7. Prepare your tee by spreading it out flat and placing some of the extra fabric or newsprint inside the tee. Doing this will prevent the paint from bleeding through to the other side of the shirt.

8. Get printing! Start at the top of your tee and work down. Reapply paint to your potato after each print.

9. Repeat with another potato stamp for more detail and to use other colors, if you wish.

10. Let the T-shirt dry.

11. Heat-set the paint according to the manufacturer's directions.

12. If you want to return to the project another day, wash off your potatoes and place them in a plastic bag. They should last a few days if they are covered.

## TIP

If you accidentally cut off part of your image when you are carving the potato, you can reattach it with a straight pin. Just make sure you don't poke yourself with the sharp edge of the pin while you're printing!

## VARIATION

Do you want to try a printing project that doesn't involve carving? You can print with any firm vegetable. Just slice the vegetable in half and use the halves as your printing surface. Try something that naturally has lots of texture, like a fennel bulb.

# Binary Code

## Binary Code

Sometimes I'm kind of lazy, and I don't want to come up with my own motifs. So for this project, I bought a numbers stamp at an office-supply store and used it to decorate my tee. To keep things simple, I didn't even use all of the numbers, just different combinations of ones and zeros. Using the stamp to create an overall fish-scales pattern gives great graphic impact. People won't know how you made this lovely tee unless they look at it closely. Then the code will be revealed!

### WHAT YOU'LL NEED

[ ] T-shirt

[ ] Extra fabric or newsprint for testing and padding

[ ] Numbers stamp or other stamp of your choice

[ ] Fabric stamp pads

## HOW TO DO IT

1. Lay the T-shirt flat on the table. Place some of the newsprint or extra fabric inside the shirt so that ink won't bleed through to the other side of the tee.

2. Select some numbers on the stamp for your code. Perhaps your high school locker combination?

3. Test your setup by inking the stamp with the stamp pads, and stamping on the test fabric. You will probably need to re-ink the stamp each time you use it.

4. Get stamping. Here's how to to create the fish-scales pattern:

   a. Starting at the bottom of the T-shirt, make each scale by stamping the numbers five or six times in a radius, keeping one end of the stamp in the same place as you go around in a circle.

   b. Do one whole row of scales across the bottom of the shirt. Then start with the next row, placing each scale in between the two below it. If you work in rows, it will be easy to keep the scales even.

5. Keep stamping until you cover the entire shirt, or stop somewhere in between if you get to something you like.

6. Let the stamp ink dry.

7. Heat-set the tee before washing and wearing.

### TIP

Don't worry too much about making little mistakes as you are stamping the pattern. Even if some of the stamping is a little bit off, it won't make much difference in the overall look of the tee.

### VARIATION

Want to send a secret message? Do it on your tee! Use online resources to translate your message into binary code, then print the message on your tee with the numbers stamp. You'll have lots of fun watching your friends try to decode it.

# Block Out

I've never actually made a quilt—I can't seem to find the time. With this project, you can quickly turn popular quilt-block motifs into printing blocks for a quilt on a tee. It's a great "quilting" option for folks like me. And carving designs into linoleum blocks is just too much fun to resist—not only do you end up with a timeless tee, but also a reusable stamp.

## WHAT YOU'LL NEED

[ ] T-shirt

[ ] Carbon paper

[ ] Pencil

[ ] Linoleum blocks—1 per color or design

[ ] Block-printing carving tools

[ ] Block-printing inks

[ ] Small sheet of glass or plexiglass

[ ] Brayer

[ ] Extra fabric or newsprint for testing and padding

## Block Out

### HOW TO DO IT

1. Enlarge or minimize the artwork provided (page 128) to the desired size, or create your own images. I made each of my blocks approximately 4" (10 cm) square. If you prefer, create your own motifs. Keep in mind that the images will print in reverse.

2. Place the artwork on top of the linoleum blocks with the carbon paper sandwiched in between.

3. Transfer the images to the printing blocks by tracing over them.

4. Carve out the blocks with the carving tools. (I use a U-shaped gouge for carving out larger areas and a V-shaped gouge for detailed areas.) Carve carefully, always aiming the carving tool away from you. (Like the potato stamps for the Totem Tee on page 46, the raised areas of the block are the parts that will print. You are carving away the areas around your artwork.) Cut down at least ¼" (5 mm) into the surface—this will make it easier to ensure that you don't accidentally get ink on areas that you don't want to print. You can also cut all of the linoleum away in some areas, if you wish. You may find it helpful to heat up the linoleum block with a heating pad or hot water bottle to make it softer and easier to carve.

5. When you have carved out all of your shapes, you're ready to get started. Place a small amount of ink on one end of your glass sheet. If you are creating a custom color, mix it right on the glass with a palette knife or a piece of cardboard.

6. Roll the ink across the glass with the brayer until it covers the brayer and gets tacky. It will sort of look like stucco.

7. Ink up your block by rolling the brayer across it a couple of times. Take care to clean up ink from any edges of the block that are not part of the raised image.

8. Flip the block ink-side down onto the test fabric. Lean into the block with the full weight of your hand.

9. Lift up the block and see what you have. Test a bit, using different amounts of ink until you get a nice print. You may want to hit the back of the block with a mallet to get more pressure or roll over it with a dry brayer if the mallet option is too noisy for you.

# PRINTING WITH LINOLEUM BLOCKS

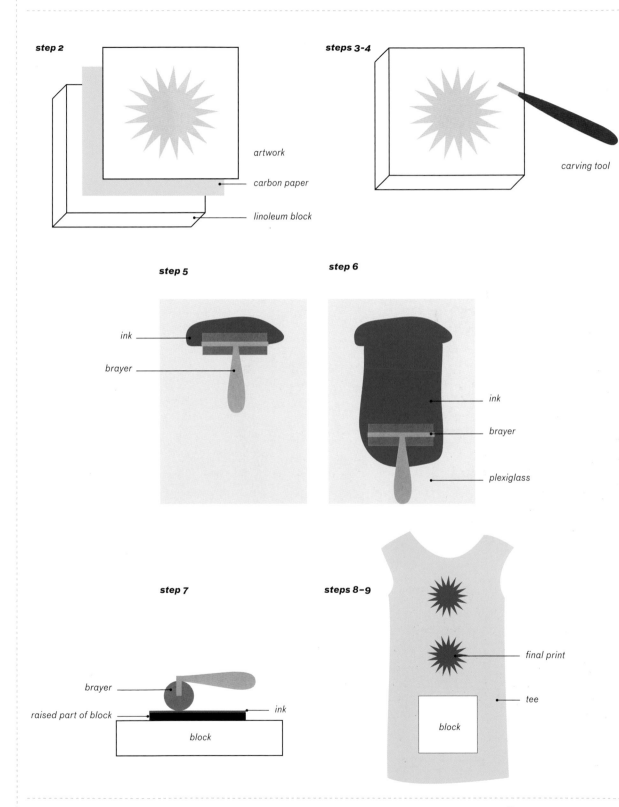

**step 2**

artwork

carbon paper

linoleum block

**steps 3-4**

carving tool

**step 5**

ink

brayer

**step 6**

ink

brayer

plexiglass

**step 7**

brayer

raised part of block

ink

block

**steps 8-9**

final print

tee

block

## Block Out

### TIP

Full disclosure here: I originally learned block printing in a fine art setting, and I personally like the consistency and texture of the traditional block-printing–oil-based inks. These can be used for fabrics, too, and can be cleaned up nicely with vegetable oil (instead of harsh mineral spirits). If you prefer to use water-based inks, use a foam brayer or small paint roller from the hardware store in place of the hard brayer that works with traditional block-printing inks. You will not be able to roll out the water-based inks with a hard brayer, because these inks are more fluid. The brayer won't roll properly, and it won't pick up the inks, which can lead to a lot of frustration.

**10.** When you're satisfied, get started on your tee. Place the extra fabric inside the T-shirt so that the ink won't bleed through to the other side, and lay your tee out flat on the table.

**11.** Print the first color.

    a. Start the quilt block pattern in one corner, printing one block and re-inking it in between each print.

    b. Use the first print to line up the second print, and so on. Since the two quilt block images are the same size, you can use the second block as a measurement guide if you want to leave open spaces in the print. If you like, you can turn the blocks as you go to get a zigzag feel, as I did.

**12.** Print the second motif and color.

**13.** Let the ink dry fully.

**14.** Heat-set your tee, and you're ready to go.

## VARIATION

At the art supply store, you will also find rubber-carving blocks next to the linoleum ones. Try them, too, if you like. They are easier to carve than linoleum, and you have the added benefit of being able to completely cut away any large sections of the block that are not part of your artwork. (This way, you don't have to worry about getting extra ink on those areas.) However, the rubber carving blocks do tend to crumble a bit around the edges, where linoleum blocks do not. Experiment to see which you prefer. For some reason, projects made with rubber blocks are called "stamping" instead of "block printing," even though the process is exactly the same.

**TECHNIQUE: Block Printing**

# Junk Print

Design inspiration is everywhere! There are so many shapes out there just waiting to be turned into patterns. I did a search around my house and found a number of interesting things that I wanted to use. I finally settled on some small bits of junk I had picked up off the street and used their shapes to create printing blocks.

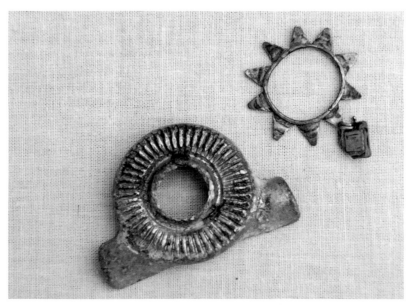

*My "junk inspiration" for this project.*

## Junk Print

### WHAT YOU'LL NEED

[ ] T-shirt

[ ] Carbon paper

[ ] Pencil

[ ] Linoleum blocks—1 per color or design

[ ] Block-printing carving tools

[ ] Block-printing inks

[ ] Small sheet of glass or plexiglass

[ ] Brayer

[ ] Extra fabric or newsprint for testing and padding

[ ] Posterboard cut ¼" (5 mm) larger than your tee

### HOW TO DO IT

**1.** Copy the images provided (page 128) and enlarge or minimize them to the desired size. If you prefer, create your own motifs. Keep in mind that your images will print in reverse.

**2.** Place the artwork on top of the linoleum blocks with the carbon paper sandwiched in between.

**3.** Transfer the images to the printing blocks by tracing over them with the pencil.

**4.** Carve out the blocks with the carving tools. I use a U-shaped gouge for carving out larger areas and a V-shaped gouge for detailed areas. Carve carefully, always aiming the carving tool away from you. (Like the potato stamps in the Totem Tee on page 46, the raised areas of the block are the parts that will print. You are carving away the areas around your artwork.) Cut down at least ¼" (5 mm) into the surface—this will make it easier to ensure that you don't accidentally get ink on areas that you don't want to print. You can also cut all of the linoleum away in some areas. You may find it helpful to heat up the linoleum block with a heating pad or hot water bottle to make it softer to carve.

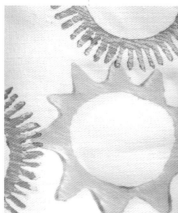

# PRINTING WITH LINOLEUM BLOCKS

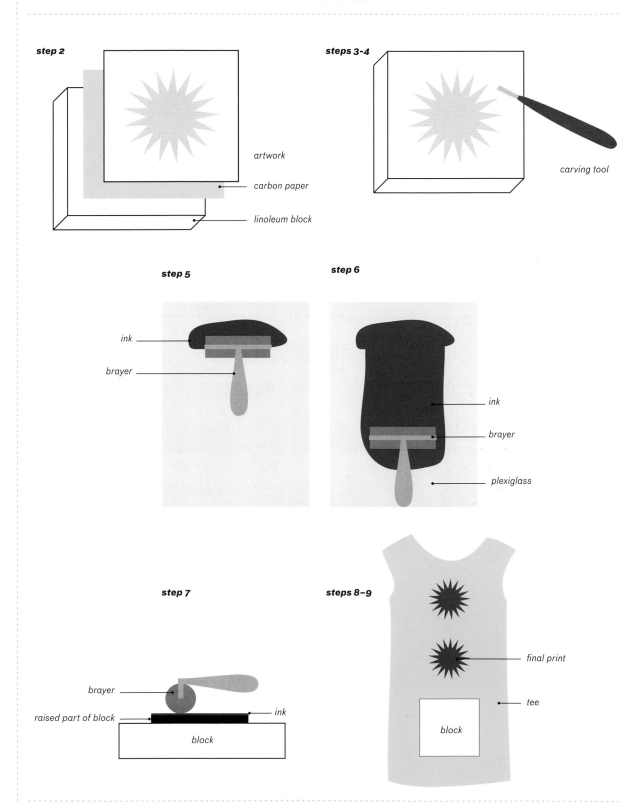

**step 2**

artwork

carbon paper

linoleum block

**steps 3-4**

carving tool

**step 5**

ink

brayer

**step 6**

ink

brayer

plexiglass

**step 7**

brayer

raised part of block

ink

block

**steps 8–9**

final print

tee

block

5. When you have carved out all of your blocks, you're ready to get started. Place a small amount of ink on one end of your glass sheet.

6. Roll the ink across the glass with the brayer until it covers the brayer and gets tacky. It will sort of look like stucco.

7. Ink up your block by rolling the brayer across it a couple of times. Take care to clean up ink from any edges of the block that are not part of the raised image.

8. Flip the block ink-side down onto your test fabric. Lean into the block with the full weight of your hand.

9. Lift up the block and see what you have. Test a bit, using different amounts of ink until you get a nice print. You may want to hit the back of the block with a mallet to get more pressure, or roll over it with a dry brayer if the mallet option is too noisy for you.

10. When you're satisfied with the print on your test fabric, get started on your tee. Place the posterboard inside the T-shirt so that the ink won't bleed through to the other side, and lay your tee flat on the table. The posterboard will also give your tee some shape and keep it very flat so that you can print all the way to the edges of the tee. I placed some fabric scraps inside the sleeves of my tee as well, which helped them lie flat while I was printing.

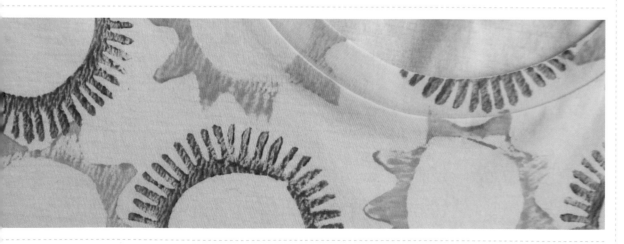

11. Print the first color. To print my alternating 3" (7.5 cm) circle images, I used a ruler as a guide. I didn't want the placement of my circles to be exact, so I didn't bother to mark everything out precisely.

  a. To use this method, place the ruler along the bottom edge of where you want to start printing, lining up the ruler with one edge of the tee.

  b. Starting from that side, print the first block and use the ruler to determine where you want your next print to be. Leave a little more space than the size of your artwork between each motif (in my case it was about 3½" or 8 cm), so that there is room to print the second block later.

  c. After you've finished the first row, measure along the side of the T-shirt to determine where you want to place the second row. You can use the circles of the first row to determine where the circles of the next row should be.

  d. Continue working like this until you've finished the prints of the first color. You will have created one color of a checkerboard pattern with this block. Be sure to re-ink the block in between each print.

12. Print the second color. This time you won't need the ruler—you can just fill in the empty spaces of your checkerboard with the second block to complete the pattern.

13. Let the ink dry completely.

14. Heat-set the tee, and you're ready to go.

## VARIATION

You can print directly with many items, too. Skip the block carving and just dip found objects directly into your inks or paints, using them as stamps like you did in the Totem Tee project (page 45). You may have to experiment to find things that print well, but it could be fun to try.

# Street Art

So many patterns can be found on the street—
literally! I love looking at all of the
lines and shapes created by road and highway
interchanges. They are great inspiration for a
rough-and-tumble, spray-painted stencil. With
this project, I kept the spray painting kind
of messy to give this tee a raw feel. And if
you are inspired by *the* street, use spray paint
to make a colorful graffiti tee.

**Street Art**

## WHAT YOU'LL NEED

[ ] Light-colored T-shirt

[ ] Acetate for cutting stencils
(1 piece per stencil color)

[ ] Pen

[ ] X-ACTO blade and cutting mat

[ ] Spray paint in a variety
of colors

[ ] Tape (masking tape
is fine for this)

[ ] Newsprint

## HOW TO DO IT

1. Enlarge or minimize the patterns provided (page 129) to the desired size, or design your own patterns.

2. Trace the patterns onto the acetate with a pen and cut out the patterns with the X-ACTO knife.

3. Lay the T-shirt out on the table. Put some newsprint between the layers of the T-shirt so no paint bleeds through to the other side. *Note: Make sure the area where you are working has good ventilation for these next steps; you may want to work outside.*

4. Place the first stencil on the T-shirt where you want it to appear, and tape it down.

5. Cover the other exposed areas of the tee with newsprint.

6. Spray the first color of paint, holding the can about 8" to 10" (20–25 cm) from the tee. Using even strokes, move the paint can across the open areas of the stencil.

7. Remove the stencil from the tee and allow it to dry completely.

8. Repeat with an additional color, if desired. *Note: I repeated each stencil twice in this project, rotating them 180 degrees for the second print.*

# PRINTING WITH STENCILS

**step 2**

**steps 3-4**

X-ACTO blade

stencil

tee

tape

stencil

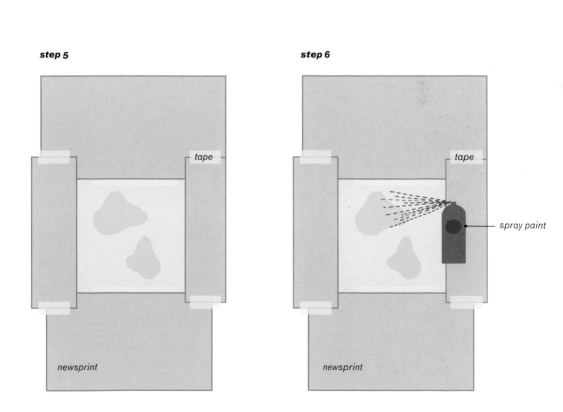

**step 5**

tape

newsprint

**step 6**

tape

spray paint

newsprint

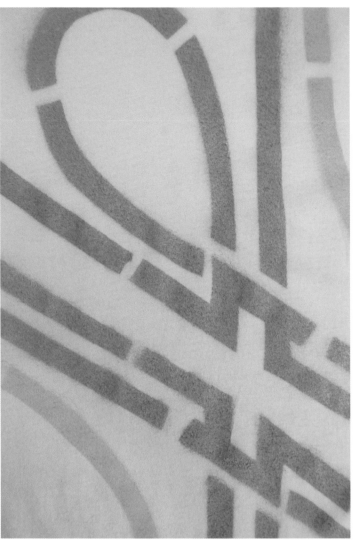

## TIP

When you're creating stencils, you need to break up long areas of your design with connecting areas of acetate; otherwise, the stencil will become too flimsy. For example, look at the stencil font used for the word "texture" on page 16; all of the letters are broken up by small connectors. Doing this properly will make your stencil stronger and much easier to work with.

## VARIATION

If you don't want to use spray paint, you can use your acetate stencil with fabric paint. Just tape the stencil to the tee and apply fabric paint with a brush.

# Geo Stripe

## Geo Stripe

Stripes are classic and pleasing to the eye. For this project, I decided to turn a conventional striped scarf into something unconventional by adding a bold geometric print. I made my print with a freezer-paper stencil, an amazingly simple yet effective technique. Create your own play on a classic stripe with just a few easy-to-find materials.

### WHAT YOU'LL NEED

[ ] Cotton striped scarf (this scarf's stripes are 1" or 2.5 cm wide)

[ ] Freezer paper

[ ] Pen

[ ] Scissors or X-ACTO knife and cutting mat

[ ] Iron

[ ] Fabric paint

[ ] Paintbrush

## Geo Stripe

### HOW TO DO IT

1. Enlarge or minimize the patterns provided (page 130) to the desired size, or design your own patterns.

2. Cut a piece of freezer paper that is 4" to 6" (10–15 cm) bigger than the size of your design. Draw your pattern in the center of it.

3. Cut out the pattern with scissors or an X-ACTO knife. I prefer an X-ACTO knife for small detail and scissors for larger areas. You will end up with a piece of freezer paper with your designs cut into it. Keep the large piece, and discard the cutout areas.

4. Spread out the scarf on your workspace. Place the freezer paper on top of it, shiny-side down.

5. Iron the paper with a dry iron so that it sticks to the fabric of the scarf.

6. Using the fabric paint and brush, paint the areas of the scarf you have cut out with the stencil. Use small strokes—it is easier to paint the fabric this way.

7. When you have filled in all of the open areas of your stencil with paint, allow the scarf to dry.

8. Carefully remove the stencil from the fabric by peeling it back evenly. Your pattern will be revealed.

9. Repeat with another color, if desired.

10. Heat-set the paint, and wrap!

### TIP

I recommend cutting a separate stencil for each color of your project, or maybe even for each individual shape. I find it more manageable to cut and position smaller pieces of freezer paper.

# PRINTING WITH FREEZER-PAPER STENCILS

**steps 2–3**

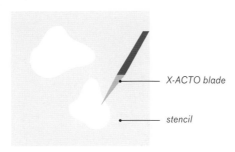

X-ACTO blade

stencil

**step 4**

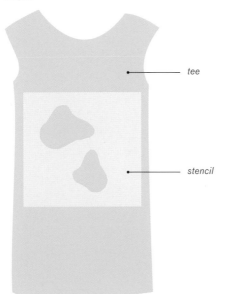

tee

stencil

**step 6**

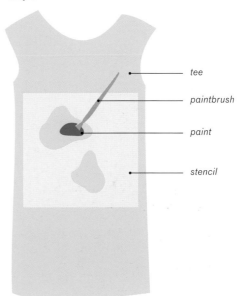

tee

paintbrush

paint

stencil

## VARIATION

Try painting *around* some shapes instead of *inside* of them. Cut out circles from freezer paper and iron them directly onto your scarf. Then start each brushstroke from the center of the circle, on top of the paper. Direct the stroke outward, toward the edge of the circle and onto the fabric. Lift the brush off the fabric slowly as you paint so the brushstroke gradually disappears. Keep going until you have outlined the entire circle in this way.

color

You've stitched, you've stamped, you've stenciled. Along the way, you've thought about how texture and pattern can be used. In this chapter, we'll look at color—undoubtedly my favorite design element! These projects play with colors in a special way, and you will take delight in how different colors interact with each other. Some use layering to great effect; others use color to define positive and negative space.

We will also focus on screen printing, the quintessential T-shirt design process. Start simply by creating basic stencils to use with your screen. Then learn some more complex techniques to create detailed silk screens that can be printed over and over. I guarantee you'll get hooked—it's impossible not to! Screen printing is a versatile process with great potential for experimentation. Soon you'll be printing everything you can get your hands on.

# SCREEN-PRINTING WORKSPACE

Fabrics are generally screen-printed on a padded work surface. They soak up more ink than paper does, and the padded surface allows you to push a bit more ink into the fabric. Use this work area for all of the screen-printing techniques outlined in this part.

## WHAT YOU'LL NEED

[ ] Table that is a comfortable height to work at while standing

[ ] Old blanket or thick felt

[ ] Muslin fabric (or other lightweight fabric)

[ ] Strong (or heavy duty) tape

[ ] Easy access to water for cleanup

## HOW TO DO IT

1. To prepare your work surface, lay the blanket or felt on the table. Smooth it out and fold it, if necessary, to create an even surface that is between $\frac{1}{8}$" (3 mm) and $\frac{1}{4}$" (5 mm) thick.

2. Place the muslin on top of the blanket, and spread it out evenly. Make sure there are no wrinkles in the fabric.

## PADDED WORK SURFACE

muslin or lightweight fabric stretched taut over table

felt or blanket

table

3. Use strong tape to attach the blanket and muslin to the table, taping evenly along all four sides of the blanket and sheet. Make sure the fabric is as taut and smooth as possible. This padded surface should be larger than your silk screen and your T-shirt, and will be your work surface. *Note: If you have a permanent worktable to devote to printing, you can attach the blanket and muslin to the table with a staple gun.*

4. Pin your T-shirts to the workspace using T-pins around the outside edges of the tee. Angle the T-pins so the points face in toward the center of the tee. Use pins at all of the corners of the shirt, and pull the shirt taut.

## TIP

To secure your T-shirts to your workspace, pin them directly to the muslin *and* felt to hold them in place while you're screen printing. It is especially important that your tee doesn't move or lift off the work surface when you pick up your screen.

## PREPARING A T-SHIRT FOR PRINTING

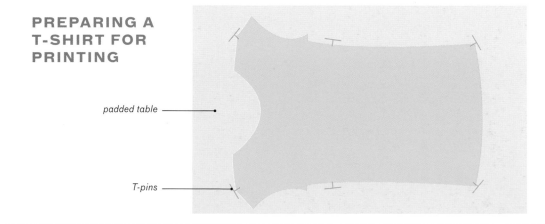

padded table —

T-pins —

# SCREEN-PRINTING TECHNIQUES

Screen printing is a stencil process. There are several ways to make a screen, and while the concept is the same, each method has different advantages. Screen fabric has natural holes in it that allow ink to pass through. You will create a design on the screen by filling in or covering some of the holes in the fabric, leaving open areas where your artwork is. Then you will pour a ribbon of ink across the edge of the screen furthest from you and pull the ink down, across your screen, with a squeegee that is larger than your artwork (for clean, even prints). The ink will flow through the open areas onto your fabric, making your print. There are three methods of screen printing presented in this part.

* Create stencils that can be applied to the screen. This method is quick and improvisational, but not well-suited to creating artwork with lots of detail. In addition, the stencils are difficult—if not impossible—to save for future projects. (See projects, pages 89–97.)

* Use a special drawing fluid and screen filler to draw or paint directly onto the screen. This method is a great option for creating long-lasting screens with a hand-drawn feel. (See projects, pages 99–107.)

* Create a screen using a photo emulsion process. This method is the industry standard and creates long-lasting screens with lots of detail, but the process takes more time and equipment to produce. (See projects, pages 109–125.)

## TIP

You should never let ink dry in your screen; it will be impossible to remove if it does dry. Always clean the screen immediately after printing. (You don't want a screen with ink on it to sit for more than two minutes.)

## Taping the Screen

It is important to tape the edges of your screens (both inside and out) with a waterproof tape before you print. This will keep ink from seeping in between the screen mesh and the frame and bleeding through the screen edges onto your project. Plus, keeping the ink contained will make it easier to collect it when you're finished printing, so you can save it for another project. The best (and most expensive) tape is a special screen-printing tape available where you purchase other printing supplies. If you're on a budget, duct or packing tape will do; just don't use it on other areas of your screen, as it will leave a sticky residue when you peel it off.

### HOW TO DO IT

1. Peel off pieces of tape the same length as the edges of your screen.

2. Place the tape along the edges where the screen and frame meet, sticking it to both the screen and frame (forming an L shape). Make sure you cover the corners, too.

3. Tape the edges on both the well side and the flat side of the screen.

### TAPING THE SCREEN

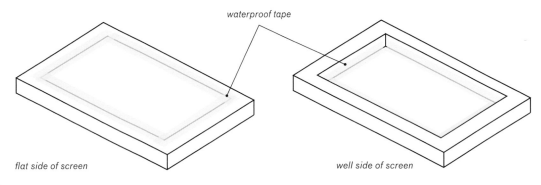

waterproof tape

flat side of screen

well side of screen

## Silk-screen Printing with Stencils

Using stencils is the most basic way of making a screen
for printing. A stencil with your design is attached to
an open screen (a screen with no image on it), and the
stencil blocks out the areas you don't want to print.
Options for making stencils include contact paper, waxed
paper, masking tape, or any kind of regular cut paper. I
love this method because it is very inexpensive, low-tech,
and spontaneous, and you can produce great, clean results
with good detail. The drawback is that it can be difficult
to preserve your stencils if you are working with paper
or tape, so you may be able to produce only a limited
amount of prints.

## APPLYING STENCILS TO THE SCREEN

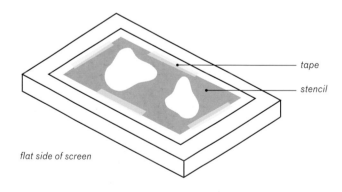

tape

stencil

flat side of screen

## Silk-screen Printing with Drawing Fluid and Screen Filler

This pair of products provides a great option to create artwork that is permanently affixed to a silk screen and has a hand-drawn feel. Basically, you apply drawing fluid to the screen with a brush to create an image that you would like to print. Then you coat the entire screen with screen filler, which fills in all of the holes in the screen mesh except the ones where the drawing fluid has been applied. Finally, you wash out the drawing fluid with water, creating open areas of the screen that will allow ink to pass through.

## CREATING A SILK SCREEN WITH SCREEN FILLER

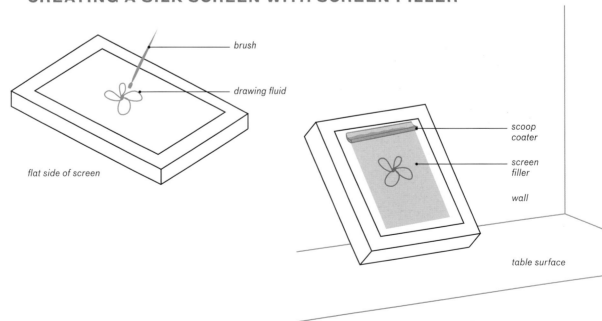

brush

drawing fluid

flat side of screen

scoop coater

screen filler

wall

table surface

# Silk-screen Printing with Photo Emulsion

The photo-emulsion process is the most common way to make screens in the industry. In order to use this method, you have to make a film positive. This is a version of your art in black on a piece of transparency film, vellum, or acetate. Each color will require a separate film positive. It's important that your artwork be very opaque in order to make a good screen. You can employ any of the following methods for making film positives.

* Draw directly on acetate, transparency film, or vellum with opaque materials (black tempera paint, paint pens, etc.).

* Photocopy your artwork onto acetate, transparency film, or vellum.

* Make a computer printout onto acetate, transparency film, or vellum.

## TIP

In screen printing, unlike some other printing processes, your art will print exactly as you create it, not in reverse. This means that you don't have to flip text to make it legible.

With any method that you choose, make sure that your artwork will fit properly in the screen that you are using. You don't want the image to come too close to the edge of the screen, so leave at least 2" (5 cm) of empty screen on all sides of your art. You will need a place for ink to collect on either side of your image. Also, the tension is best in the center of the screen, so you will get a better print if you center your artwork.

## WHAT YOU'LL NEED

[ ] Acetate, transparency film, or vellum

[ ] Photo emulsion for water-based inks (sensitizer comes with the emulsion)

[ ] Silk screen with an open mesh (110 for fabric printing) that is large enough to accommodate your artwork and leave 2" (5 cm) of space around the art on all sides

[ ] Scoop coater or squeegee

[ ] Fan (optional)

[ ] Light source such as a 250-watt photoflood bulb

[ ] Foam that fits snugly underneath the screen (optional)

[ ] Black paper that is larger than your artwork (optional)

[ ] Piece of glass that is larger than your artwork

[ ] Scrub brush

## EXPOSING SILK SCREEN SETUP, 2 VIEWS

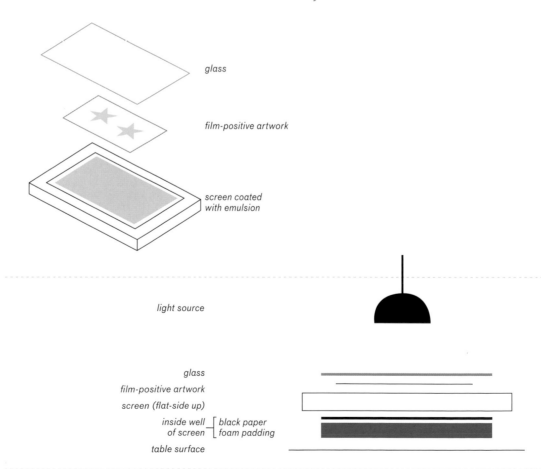

glass

film-positive artwork

screen coated with emulsion

light source

glass
film-positive artwork
screen (flat-side up)
inside well of screen — black paper / foam padding
table surface

## HOW TO DO IT

1. Photocopy the artwork from this book (see Templates, page 126) onto a piece of clear acetate, transparency film, or vellum. The copy must be very dark—all black areas should be opaque. If you cannot get a dark enough copy, you can make two copies and layer them together, making sure you line up the artwork precisely. *Note: If you want to create your own artwork, make sure you use only black and white in your image. Shades of gray will* not *print. A black-and-white photograph, for example, has too many gray tones to make a good stencil.*

2. Working in a darkened room, mix the sensitizer with the photo emulsion according to the manufacturer's directions. The room does not have to be a full darkroom; there should be enough light to see what you're doing, but not enough to read or write by. (Photo emulsion is not as sensitive as typical photo-processing chemistry.)

3. Lean your screen at a 45-degree angle against a wall.

4. Apply a ribbon of emulsion to the well of the scoop coater, and place the scoop coater along the bottom edge of the screen.

5. Holding the scoop coater at a 45-degree angle and, keeping it pressed firmly against the screen, draw upward, leaving a very thin film of emulsion on the screen.

6. Repeat this process on the other side of the screen. It is very important that the emulsion stays smooth—a thick coat will make it difficult to expose the screen properly. Wipe up any drips along the edges of the screen with a small piece of cardboard. Do not touch the wet emulsion in the center of the screen.

*steps 3–5* **APPLYING PHOTO EMULSION**

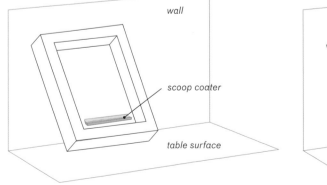

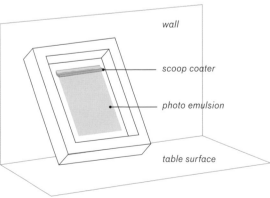

7. Leave the screen to dry. You can use a fan to speed up the drying. Do not proceed to the next step until the screen is fully dry.

8. Hang the light source so it points directly down onto the table. The distance of the light source from the screen will affect the exposure time, as will the size of the screen and artwork. A closer light source will shorten exposure time. Make sure that the light shines evenly on all areas of the screen. The manufacturer of the photo emulsion should provide a timetable/distance chart.

9. Place the foam on the table underneath the light source and place the black paper on top of the foam.

10. Place the coated silk screen on top of the paper, with the flat side facing up. The foam and paper should fill up the well of the screen and touch the back side of the screen. This will provide good pressure against the glass in the next steps.

11. Place the film-positive artwork in the center of the screen. You can hold it in place with a few pieces of clear tape. *Note: The artwork should be oriented so that when you place the film positive on the table as you would like it to appear, and place the unexposed silk screen flat-side down on top of it, you can see the artwork correctly through the screen. (Artwork should appear correctly when viewing the screen from the well side.)*

12. Place the glass on top of the image to hold it firmly in place. All of these layers should keep your film positive touching the screen surface.

## TIP

You can use a squeegee for applying emulsion, but it is much easier to get a thin coating with a scoop coater.

13. Turn on the light and expose the film for the desired time. The emulsion manufacturer should supply a chart of exposure times based on the size of the screen, the particular light source, and the distance of the light source from the screen. You will definitely have to do some testing to figure out what works for you, as every small variable in your setup can change the exposure time. Both under- and overexposure will result in poor screen quality. So test, test, test!

14. Remove the screen from the setup, and bring it to a sink or bathtub. Use a spray nozzle to coat both sides of the screen with water. If you have enough water pressure, you can clean out the areas of the artwork with just water. You may also want to use a gentle scrub brush to get the emulsion out of the screen. Don't scrub too much or too hard. You don't want to remove all of the emulsion; it is delicate when wet.

15. When you have cleaned out all the areas of the artwork, hold the screen up to a light source and make sure you can see through the screen in these areas. These open areas of the screen will allow ink to pass through when you print. When the screen is dry, fill in any pinholes with more emulsion.

16. Allow the screen to dry overnight.

17. Before you start printing, tape the edges of the screen (both inside and out) with a waterproof tape (page 79).

**TIP**

When you are finished with a project, you can remove the photo emulsion from the screen so that you can use the screen for another project. Use an emulsion remover and apply it according to the manufacturer's directions. Just remember to keep your film positives in case you ever want to use them for another project.

### TIP

If you want to print with photo-based silk screens but don't have the inclination to make the screens yourself, there are places that will make the silk screens for you. It will cost you a little more money, but it will leave you with more time to work on printing. I recommend first talking to local T-shirt printing businesses—they have professional equipment to create your film positives and to expose silk screens. They may not generally provide silk-screen exposure as a service, but many will create some screens for you to help you out. If you can't find anyone locally, there are places where you can send artwork, and they will send back your completed screens. (See Resources, page 140, for more information.)

# OFFice DOTS

With this spontaneous method of silk-screen printing, you can use virtually anything flat as a stencil with an open silk screen. Here, I used stickers bought at an office-supply store to create a simple, graphic pattern. With this stencil method, any areas of the screen that I covered with the dot stickers did not print; instead, the areas around my stickers printed. Use negative space to your advantage and create a dotty tank top for yourself, too!

## Office Dots

### WHAT YOU'LL NEED

[ ] Light-colored tank top

[ ] Round stickers and loose-leaf paper reinforcements

[ ] Scrap paper

[ ] Silk screen with 110 mesh

[ ] Masking tape

[ ] Waterproof tape or packing tape

[ ] Prepared screen-printing workspace (page 76)

[ ] Scrap fabric

[ ] T-pins

[ ] Transparent screen-printing ink

[ ] Squeegee

### HOW TO DO IT

1. Tape the inside and outside edges of the screen with waterproof tape (page 79).

2. Design a pattern you like that incorporates the stickers and the loose-leaf reinforcements. Plan it out in a drawing, or make a test layout with the stickers on a scrap piece of paper. I decided on a simple fan pattern radiating from the neckline of my tee. *Note: You are printing the negative space around the dots in this project; the dots themselves won't print.*

3. When you have a layout that you like, you are ready to make your screen. Place the screen flat-side up on the table.

4. Stick the dot stickers and reinforcements to the screen in your pattern. *Note: Any time you attach stencils to a silk screen you must attach them to the flat side of the screen (not the well side). This way they won't get dragged out of place by the squeegee.*

5. Mask out the remaining areas of the screen. Create a box around your dot artwork with scrap paper, and tape the edges around the artwork firmly with masking tape. You are defining a print area when you do this, so work neatly.

*steps 3–5* APPLYING STENCILS TO THE SCREEN

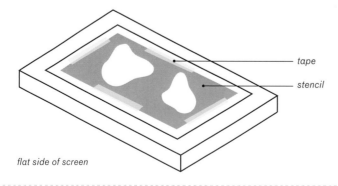

tape

stencil

*flat side of screen*

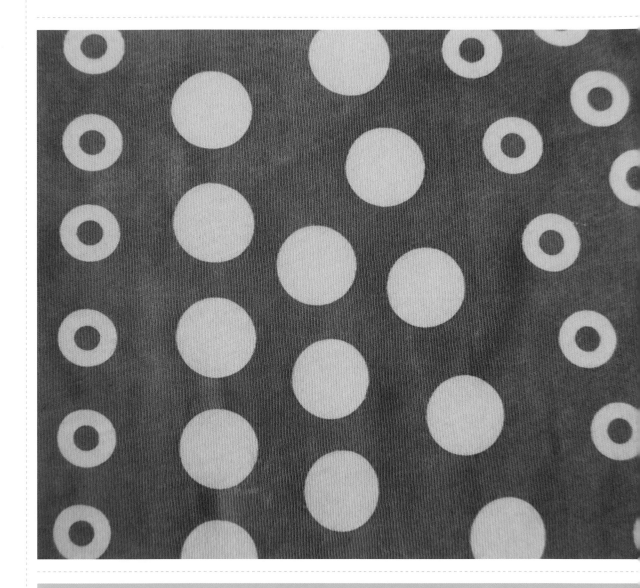

6. Cover your padded worktable with a scrap piece of fabric, as the ink will run off of the edge of the tee with this project. Use T-pins to attach the scrap fabric.

7. Pin the tee to the worktable on top of the scrap fabric.

8. Now you are ready to print. Arrange the silk screen flat-side down on top of the tee.

9. Pour a ribbon of ink along the edge of the screen furthest from you.

10. Holding the screen firmly in place and the squeegee at a 45-degree angle, pull the ink across the screen with the squeegee.

11. After you have made one pass across the screen, pick up the squeegee and place it down again at the far edge. Make another pass or two with the squeegee in this manner. (With a little experimenting, you will figure out how many passes of ink you need to get a good print—I usually make three passes for T-shirts or knit fabrics.)

12. Carefully lift the screen off of the tee.

13. Allow the tee to dry.

14. Heat-set the fabric.

## VARIATION

Masking tape is a great material to use in place of stickers for this project. Find different widths of tape and create a fan pattern, using lengths of tape radiating out from a center point.

# POSITIVE NEGATIVE

## Positive Negative

In this project, you are screen-printing with bleach to remove color from a dark T-shirt. Bleach printing is great because the fabric stays very smooth since you are not adding anything to the tee. Plus, it has a distinct rock-and-roll vibe. I created a detailed geometric stencil for my graphic. My T-shirt fabric bleached to a fabulous reddish color, which I love. All fabrics take bleach differently (and some, not at all), so experiment to find something you like.

## WHAT YOU'LL NEED

[ ] Dark-colored T-shirt

[ ] Waxed paper or freezer paper

[ ] X-ACTO knife and cutting mat

[ ] Waterproof tape or packing tape

[ ] Silk screen with 110 mesh

[ ] Masking tape

[ ] Newsprint

[ ] Prepared screen-printing workspace (page 76)

[ ] T-pins

[ ] Bleach

[ ] Bleach thickener

[ ] Squeegee

[ ] Bleach-stop (optional)

## HOW TO DO IT

1. Enlarge or minimize the artwork provided (page 131) to the desired size, or create your own image.

2. Cut out the stencil.

   a. Tape the paper with the artwork to the cutting mat.

   b. Tape a piece of waxed paper or freezer paper on top, so the artwork is visible underneath.

   c. Using the artwork as a guide, carefully cut out the stencil from the freezer or waxed paper with an X-ACTO knife. You will also cut through the paper with the artwork on it—this is fine, you won't need it later. If you prefer, you can trace the artwork onto the freezer paper first so you don't have to use the artwork itself as a cutting guide.

3. Tape the inside and outside edges of the screen with waterproof tape (page 79).

4. Attach your stencil to the flat side of the silk screen with masking tape.

5. Cover up any open areas of the screen around the stencil with additional freezer paper and masking tape. When you are finished, the only open areas of the screen should be the cutouts of the stencil.

6. Place the newsprint inside the T-shirt to keep bleach from leaking through to the other side of the shirt, and pin the T-shirt to the table with T-pins at your prepared workspace.

7. Mix the bleach thickener with the bleach according to the manufacturer's directions, using the proportions listed for screen printing. *Note: Make sure the*

*steps 4–5* **APPLYING STENCILS TO THE SCREEN**

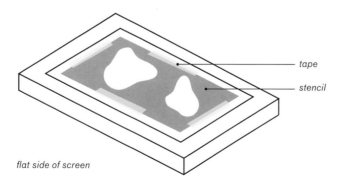

tape

stencil

*flat side of screen*

### TIP

Bleach thickener can be purchased at suppliers of fabric paints and dyes. Bleach alone is too liquid to screen-print well. The thickener is a *vehicle* for the bleach—it creates the right consistency for the bleach to be used as printing ink.

*area where you are working has good ventilation for these next steps; you may want to work outside. Also, wear the proper protective clothing when working with a chemical like bleach.*

8. Place the silk screen flat-side down on top of the T-shirt on your prepared workspace.

9. Using the bleach solution as you would printing ink, pour a ribbon of bleach solution along the edge of the screen furthest from you.

10. Holding the screen firmly in place and the squeegee at a 45-degree angle, pull the bleach solution across the screen with the squeegee.

11. After you have made one pass across the screen, pick up the squeegee and place it down again at the far edge. Make another few passes with the squeegee in this manner. The more bleach you get through the screen, the more potential you have for removing the color from the T-shirt.

12. Lift the screen off the T-shirt and remove the stencil from the screen. It can be difficult to keep the stencil intact, but if you are careful, you can save it to use again later.

13. Wash off the screen.

14. Remove the T-shirt from the table and take out the newsprint.

15. Rinse out the T-shirt to remove any additional bleach from the image area. You can use bleach-stop to end the bleaching action, if necessary. (Bleach can just go on and on beaching if you let it.)

16. Let the T-shirt dry, and you're ready to go!

## TIP

Sometimes, I use this little trick: Instead of buying bleach and thickener separately, I buy a bathroom tile cleanser with bleach added. I use the cleanser in place of the bleach/thickener mixture, and print with it as I would with any other ink. The cleanser takes the place of bleach thickener; it's the right consistency for printing. It's also easy to find at your local grocery store.

# THe scriBBLe

If you are in need of inspiration for your tee designs, look no further than the doodles you make while talking on the phone. For this tee, I made a simple graphic by sketching rows of dotted circles. Then I transferred my drawing to a silk screen with screen-drawing fluid, and printed the screen with gold ink. The result: a sparkly, delicate pattern with lots of sketchy style.

## The Scribble

### WHAT YOU'LL NEED

[ ] T-shirt

[ ] Masking tape

[ ] Silk screen with 110 mesh

[ ] Paintbrush

[ ] Screen-drawing fluid

[ ] Screen filler

[ ] Scoop coater (optional)

[ ] Waterproof tape or packing tape

[ ] Newsprint

[ ] Prepared screen-printing workspace (page 76)

[ ] T-pins

[ ] Screen-printing ink

[ ] Squeegee

### HOW TO DO IT

1. Enlarge or minimize the artwork provided (page 132) to the desired size, or create your own image.

2. With the masking tape, attach the artwork to the silk screen on the well side of the screen. Position the paper so that you can see the image when looking through the screen from the flat side.

3. Place the silk screen well-side down on the table. You will be able to see the artwork on the paper underneath the screen.

4. Using the artwork as a guide, copy it onto the screen with screen-drawing fluid and a paintbrush. If you wish, you can skip using the guide and just paint freehand directly onto the screen.

5. When you have completed your design, allow the drawing fluid to dry completely and remove the artwork guide.

6. Coat the screen with screen filler. It is possible to use a squeegee for this step, but I prefer to use a scoop coater to apply the screen filler because it goes on smoother and thinner.

   a. To do this, lean the screen against the wall at a 45-degree angle.

   b. Fill the scoop coater with screen filler, and lean it against the bottom of the screen.

   c. Tilt the scoop coater at a 45-degree angle, so that the screen filler touches the screen.

   d. Drag the scoop coater evenly upward, holding it firmly against the screen. It will leave a thin film of screen filler across the screen.

   e. Fill in any open areas around the edges of the screen with additional screen filler by using a small piece of cardboard to apply it. You do not want any open areas of the screen except for the area occupied by the artwork.

7. Allow the screen to dry in a horizontal position.

8. When the screen is completely dry, wash it with cold water. The drawing fluid will wash away, leaving open areas of the screen where you applied it. You may need to rub the screen gently with a sponge to loosen the drawing fluid.

9. Allow the screen to dry completely.

10. Tape the inside and outside edges of your screen with waterproof tape (page 79).

11. Place the newsprint inside your T-shirt, and pin the T-shirt to the table with T-pins at your prepared workspace.

*steps 3–6* **CREATING A SILK SCREEN WITH SCREEN FILLER**

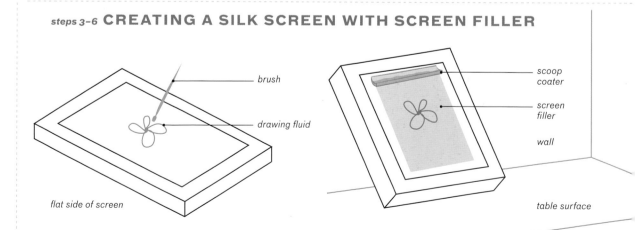

brush

drawing fluid

flat side of screen

scoop coater

screen filler

wall

table surface

## The Scribble

12. Place the silk screen on top of your tee with the flat side down, arranging it where you would like to print the artwork.

13. When the screen is in place, pour a ribbon of ink along the edge of the screen furthest from you.

14. Holding the screen firmly in place and the squeegee at a 45-degree angle, pull the ink across the screen with the squeegee.

15. After you have made one pass across the screen, pick up the squeegee and place it down again at the far edge of the screen. Make another pass or two with the squeegee in this manner. (With a little experimenting, you will figure out how many passes of ink you need to get a good print—I usually make three passes for T-shirts or knit fabrics.)

16. Lift the screen off the T-shirt.

17. Remove the extra ink from the screen and return it to the container. Then clean the screen and squeegee thoroughly with water.

18. Allow the tee to dry.

19. Heat-set your tee, and you're ready to go!

### TIP

I printed my image four times on this tee. To do this, print the first print, then lift the screen off of the tee and place it to the side for a moment. Put a piece of scrap paper over your first print so that the ink from that print won't get smudged. Then place the silk screen on top of your tee where you want the next print to go. Print the image again, and repeat. Alternately, you can clean the screen after each print, and print again when the screen and tee are dry.

### VARIATION

This method of screen preparation works very well with loose, brushstroke-y images. Take the title of this project literally, and scribble with drawing fluid directly onto your screen. You will end up with an image that is spontaneous and lively—perfect for printing on a tee.

# two for one

**Two for One**

I love collage, so I decided to create a tee out of it! First I printed two T-shirts, both with the same flower image. Then I cut each tee in half and switched them to create an entirely new tee. The print by itself is great, but the addition of the collage element makes it a lot more fun.

## WHAT YOU'LL NEED

[ ] 2 T-shirts of the same size

[ ] Masking tape

[ ] Silk screen with 110 mesh

[ ] Paintbrush

[ ] Screen-drawing fluid

[ ] Screen filler

[ ] Scoop coater (optional)

[ ] Waterproof tape or packing tape

[ ] Newsprint

[ ] Prepared screen-printing workspace (page 76)

[ ] T-pins

[ ] Screen-printing ink

[ ] Squeegee

[ ] Fan (optional)

[ ] Rag

[ ] Sewing machine or serger

## HOW TO DO IT

1. Enlarge or minimize the artwork provided (page 133) to the desired size, or create your own image.

2. With the masking tape, attach the artwork to the silk screen on the well side of the screen. Position the paper so that you can see the image when looking through the screen from the flat side.

3. Place the silk screen well-side down on the table.

4. Using the artwork as a guide, copy it onto the screen with screen-drawing fluid and the paintbrush. If you wish, you can skip using the guide and just paint freehand directly onto the screen.

5. When you have completed your design, allow the drawing fluid to dry completely and remove the artwork guide.

6. Coat the screen with screen filler. It is possible to use a squeegee for this step, but I prefer to use a scoop coater to apply the screen filler because it goes on smoother and thinner.

   a. To do this, lean the screen against the wall at a 45-degree angle.

   b. Fill the scoop coater with screen filler, and lean it against the bottom of the screen.

   c. Tilt the scoop coater at a 45-degree angle, so that the screen filler touches the screen.

   d. Drag the scoop coater evenly upward, holding it firmly against the screen. It will leave a thin film of screen filler across the screen.

*steps 3–6* **CREATING A SILK SCREEN WITH SCREEN FILLER**

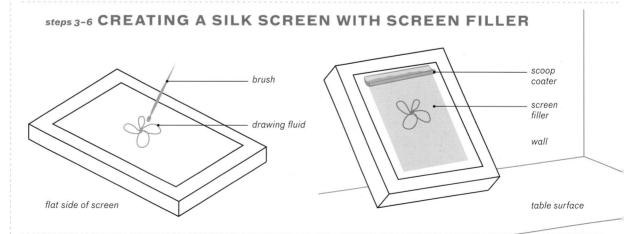

brush

drawing fluid

flat side of screen

scoop coater

screen filler

wall

table surface

    e. Fill in any open areas around the edges of the screen with additional screen filler by using a small piece of cardboard to apply it. You do not want any open areas of the screen except for the area occupied by the artwork.

**7.** Allow the screen to dry in a horizontal position.

**8.** When the screen is completely dry, wash it with cold water. The drawing fluid will wash away, leaving open areas of the screen where you had applied it. You may need to rub the screen gently with a sponge to loosen the drawing fluid.

**9.** Allow the screen to dry completely.

**10.** Tape the inside and outside edges of your screen with waterproof tape (page 79).

**11.** Place the newsprint inside the first T-shirt, and pin the tee to the table with T-pins at your prepared workspace.

**12.** Place the silk screen on top of your tee with the flat side down, arranging it where you would like to print the artwork.

13. When the screen is in place, pour a ribbon of ink along the edge of the screen furthest from you.

14. Holding the screen firmly in place and the squeegee at a 45-degree angle, pull the ink across the screen with the squeegee.

15. After you have made one pass across the screen, pick up the squeegee and place it down again at the far edge. Make another pass or two with the squeegee in this manner. (With a little experimenting, you will figure out how many passes of ink you need to get a good print—I usually make three passes for T-shirts or knit fabrics.)

16. Lift the screen off the T-shirt.

17. Remove the extra ink from the screen and return it to the container. Then clean the screen and squeegee thoroughly with water.

18. While your T-shirt is drying, you can place the silk screen in front of a fan to dry it out so that you can print your next color. Make sure the screen is completely dry before you print again—any water left on the screen or squeegee can mix with the inks and ruin your print. Use a rag to dry off the edges of the screen or the squeegee, if necessary.

19. Repeat steps 12 through 18 with the second T-shirt. Allow the tee to dry.

20. Heat-set the tees.

21. Lay both tees flat on the table, and cut them in half horizontally.

22. Using a serger or sewing machine set to zigzag stitch, sew the opposite halves together at the cut edge, using a ¼" (5 mm) seam allowance. I decided to leave the seam on the outside of the tee for added punch.

## TIP

Try to keep the drawing fluid from getting too thick when you are painting the screen. Very thick areas can get crusty and keep the screen filler from adhering properly. When this happens, you can accidentally wash away part of your image when you wash the drawing fluid out of the screen.

## VARIATION

Try printing one of your tees with a screen from another project, so each tee has a different graphic. When you sew these tees together, your tee collage will have added dimension.

# FLIP SIDE

Try something subtle by using your silk screen to make a tonal print. Then rotate the image and print it again in a contrasting color. I've taken a fern graphic and printed it with opaque white ink on a white tee to create depth. I printed the same image again in bright orange to create a punchy complement to my white-on-white graphic.

## WHAT YOU'LL NEED

[ ] White T-shirt

[ ] Waterproof tape or packing tape

[ ] Newsprint

[ ] Silk screen with 110 mesh

[ ] Prepared screen-printing workspace (page 76)

[ ] T-pins

[ ] Screen-printing ink

[ ] Squeegee

[ ] Fan (optional)

[ ] Rag

## HOW TO DO IT

1. Enlarge or minimize the artwork provided (page 134) to the desired size, or create your own image.

2. Expose the silk screen with the artwork, using the photo-emulsion technique described on page 82.

3. When the screen is exposed and dry, tape the inside and outside edges of the screen with waterproof tape (page 79).

4. Put newsprint inside the T-shirt to keep ink from bleeding through the shirt to the other side, and pin the tee to your prepared workspace using T-pins.

5. Place the silk screen on top of your tee with the flat side down, arranging it where you would like to print the white fern image.

6. When the screen is in place, pour a ribbon of ink along the edge of the screen furthest from you.

7. Holding the screen firmly in place and the squeegee at a 45-degree angle, pull the ink across the screen with the squeegee.

8. After you have made one pass across the screen, pick up the squeegee and place it down again at the far edge. Make another pass or two with the squeegee in this manner. (With a little experimenting, you will figure out how many passes of ink you need to get a good print—I usually make three passes for T-shirts or knit fabrics.)

### TIP

Opaque inks, like the white used in this project, are thicker than transparent ones. You may have to press harder with your squeegee or make additional passes to get good coverage with these thick inks. They can also start to dry in the screen while you're working. If you're really having trouble getting a good print, try using retarder, an additive that slows down the drying time of your ink, making it easier to print without the ink clogging up your screen.

**9.** Lift the screen off the T-shirt.

**10.** Remove the extra ink from the screen and return it to the container. Then clean the screen and squeegee thoroughly with water.

**11.** While your T-shirt is drying, you can place the silk screen in front of a fan to dry it out so that you can print your next color. Make sure the screen is completely dry before you print again—any water left on the screen or squeegee can mix with the inks and ruin your print. Use a rag to dry off the edges of the screen or the squeegee, if necessary.

**12.** When the screen and tee are thoroughly dry, place the screen flat-side down on top of the tee, orienting the artwork in the opposite direction from the first print.

**13.** Print the screen a second time, using the colored ink.

**14.** Lift the screen off the T-shirt.

**15.** Remove the extra ink from the screen and return it to the container. Then clean the screen and squeegee thoroughly with water.

**16.** Allow the tee to dry.

**17.** Heat-set, and you're good to go.

## VARIATION

Try an experiment: See what happens if you print your bright color first, then print a white image on top of it. The bright image may show through the white a teeny bit, or parts of it may seem to disappear beneath the white. When layering colors, the order in which you print them can make a huge difference in the look of the final design.

# sLeek sLeeves

## Sleek Sleeves

You can use all of the surfaces of your shirt for printing: the collar, bottom hem, the back, even the cuffs. For this project, I covered the sleeves of my tee with color and pattern. The resulting tee is great for layering under a sweater vest in chilly weather. Plus, the unexpected placement of the print makes it an exciting and unusual addition to your tee wardrobe.

## WHAT YOU'LL NEED

[ ] Long-sleeved T-shirt

[ ] Silk screen with 110 mesh

[ ] Waterproof tape or packing tape

[ ] Posterboard

[ ] Scissors

[ ] Prepared screen-printing workspace (page 76)

[ ] T-pins

[ ] Screen-printing ink

[ ] Squeegee

## HOW TO DO IT

1. Enlarge or minimize the artwork provided (page 135) to the desired size, or create your own image. You want the artwork to cover the sleeves, so measure the sleeves of the shirt first and make sure the art fits.

2. Using the instructions for the photo-emulsion technique on page 82, expose the silk screen for this project.

3. When the screen is exposed and dry, tape the inside and outside edges of the screen with waterproof tape (page 79).

4. Cut two pieces of posterboard that are about ¾" (2 cm) wider than the sleeves of your shirt and longer than your artwork. Place these inside the sleeves. They will help keep the ink from bleeding through the tee and make the sleeves stiff so they are easier to handle when they are wet. You want the fabric of the shirt to be tight around the posterboard.

5. Lay the T-shirt out on the prepared work surface. Place one sleeve on the table and pin it to the padded muslin with the T-pins, being careful to point the pins toward the center of the shirt so they don't pull out accidentally while you are working.

6. Place the silk screen flat-side down on the first sleeve, lining up the artwork where you would like it to appear on the sleeve.

7. When the screen is in place, pour a ribbon of ink along the edge of the screen furthest from you.

**Sleek Sleeves**

**8.** Holding the screen firmly in place and the squeegee at a 45-degree angle, pull the ink across the screen with the squeegee.

**8.** After you have made one pass across the screen, pick up the squeegee and place it down again at the far edge. Make another pass or two with the squeegee in this manner. (With a little experimenting, you will figure out how many passes of ink you need to get a good print—I usually make three passes for T-shirts or knit fabrics.)

**9.** Lift the screen off the T-shirt.

**10.** Remove the extra ink from the screen and return it to the container. Then clean the screen and squeegee thoroughly with water.

**11.** When the T-shirt is dry to the touch, unpin the sleeve of the T-shirt from the table.

**12.** Repeat steps 5 through 11, printing the pattern on the second sleeve.

**13.** Print the back sides of the sleeves in the same manner in a different color, if desired.

**14.** Heat-set your tee after it is completely dry.

**TIP**

I prefer to use rib-knit tees for this project. Since you are printing off the edge of the fabric, you can affect the stretchability of the knit fabric; the extra stretch of a rib knit helps the arms of the tee to keep their shape. Flat-knit tees can get really stretched out with this technique. If you use opaque inks as I have here, expect the printed area of the tee to be a bit stiff when you first make it. After a few days of washing and wearing, the inks will get very soft.

**VARIATION**

Want your legs to be as patterned as your arms? Print yourself a pair of knee socks! Use the same process as described here, putting posterboard inside the legs of the socks. Then proceed with the printing the same way you would print the sleeves of a tee.

# DOUBLeVISION

## Double Vision

I find that 3-D images look more interesting without the 3-D glasses—separated into their red and blue components. So I made a tee that looks like it *could* be a 3-D image. I chose an image with lots of detail to accentuate the overlapping colors, creating three-dimensional interest with a two-dimensional graphic.

### WHAT YOU'LL NEED

[ ] White- or natural-colored T-shirt

[ ] Silk screen with 110 mesh

[ ] Waterproof tape or packing tape

[ ] Newsprint

[ ] Prepared screen-printing workspace (page 76)

[ ] T-pins

[ ] Screen-printing ink in cyan blue and medium red

[ ] Squeegee

[ ] Fan (optional)

[ ] Rag

## HOW TO DO IT

1. Enlarge or minimize the artwork provided (page 136) to the desired size, or create your own image.

2. Expose the silk screen, using the photo-emulsion technique described on page 82.

3. When the screen is exposed and dry, tape the inside and outside edges of the screen with waterproof tape (page 79).

4. Place newsprint inside the T-shirt to keep ink from bleeding through the shirt to the other side, and pin the tee to the prepared workspace using T-pins.

5. Place the silk screen on top of the tee with the flat side down, arranging it where you would like to print the 3-D image.

6. When the screen is in place, pour a ribbon of blue ink along the edge of the screen furthest from you.

7. Holding the screen firmly in place and the squeegee at a 45-degree angle, pull the ink across the screen with the squeegee.

8. After you have made one pass across the screen, pick up the squeegee and place it down again at the far edge. Make another pass or two with the squeegee in this manner. (With a little experimenting, you will figure out how many passes of ink you need to get a good print—I usually make three passes for T-shirts or knit fabrics.)

9. Lift the screen off the T-shirt.

## TIP

You probably won't be able to register the second print exactly on top of the first one, so don't get frustrated trying! It is the nature of fabric to move and stretch slightly, just enough that you may be able to line up one part of your print evenly but not another. The imperfect alignment will just add depth to this project, so it works to your advantage here.

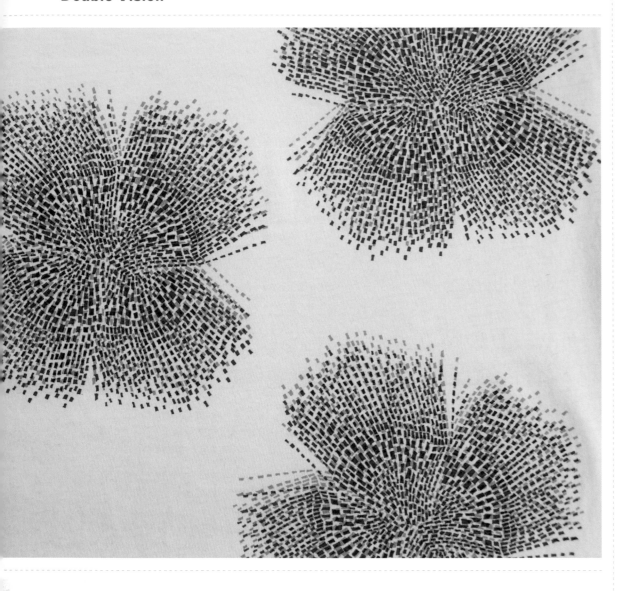

10. Remove the extra ink from the screen and return it to the container. Then clean the screen and squeegee thoroughly with water.

11. While your T-shirt is drying, you can place the silk screen in front of a fan to dry it out so that you can print the next color. Make sure the screen is completely dry before you print again—any water left on the screen or squeegee can mix with the inks and ruin the print. Use a rag to dry off the edges of the screen or the squeegee, if necessary.

12. When the screen and tee are thoroughly dry, place the screen flat-side down on top of the tee, positioning the 3-D artwork on top of the first print so that they are offset a little bit.

13. Print the screen a second time, using the red ink.

14. Lift the screen off the T-shirt.

15. Remove the extra ink from the screen and return it to the container. Then clean the screen and squeegee thoroughly with water.

16. Allow the tee to dry.

17. Heat-set your tee, and find yourself a pair of 3-D glasses!

## VARIATION

Instead of printing blue and red, try printing two versions of the same color, like two shades of green. Print the second color just slightly off from the first so the colors blend together to create an optical illusion.

# CHErry BLOSSOM

Now that you're printing like a pro, it's time to do my favorite kind of screen printing—one that uses tonal colors and layered patterns to create an image with lots of depth. For this project, create two silk screens: one with a graphic of segmented circles and one with an expanding cherry blossom. Print one of these on top of the other, and you will have a stunning tee that is rich and complex.

**WHAT YOU'LL NEED**

[ ] T-shirt

[ ] 2 silk screens with 110 mesh

[ ] Waterproof tape or packing tape

[ ] Newsprint

[ ] Prepared screen-printing workspace (page 76)

[ ] T-pins

[ ] Screen-printing ink in two colors

[ ] Squeegee

## Cherry Blossom

### HOW TO DO IT

1. Enlarge or minimize the artwork provided (pages 137–138) to the desired size, or create your own images.

2. Expose the silk screens, using the photo-emulsion technique described on page 82.

3. When the screens are exposed and dry, tape the inside and outside edges of the screens with waterproof tape (page 79).

4. Place newsprint inside the T-shirt to keep ink from bleeding through the shirt to the other side, and pin the tee to the prepared workspace using T-pins.

5. Place the first silk screen (the circles art, page 137) on top of the tee with the flat side down, arranging it where you would like to print the image.

6. When the screen is in place, pour a ribbon of ink along the edge of the screen furthest from you.

7. Holding the screen firmly in place and the squeegee at a 45-degree angle, pull the ink across the screen with the squeegee.

8. After you have made one pass across the screen, pick up the squeegee and place it down again at the far edge. Make another pass or two with the squeegee in this manner. (With a little experimenting, you will figure out how many passes of ink you need to get a good print—I usually make three passes for T-shirts or knit fabrics.)

9. Lift the screen off the T-shirt.

10. Remove the extra ink from the screen and return it to the container. Then clean the screen and squeegee thoroughly with water.

11. When the tee is thoroughly dry, place the second screen (the cherry blossom art, page 138) flat-side down on top of the tee, positioning the artwork as you would like it on top of the first print.

12. Print the second screen, using a different color of ink.

13. Lift the screen off the T-shirt.

14. Remove the extra ink from the screen, and return it to the container. Then clean the screen and squeegee thoroughly with water.

15. Allow the tee to dry.

16. Heat-set, and wear your tee in the springtime!

# Templates

The following pages contain the artwork used in the projects throughout the book. Photocopy (or trace) these templates to the desired size.

**Heirloom Star** (page 21)

100%
actual size

**Rough Edges** (page 24)

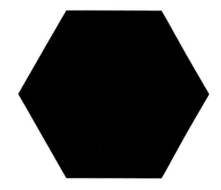

100%
actual size

**Totem Tee** (page 45)

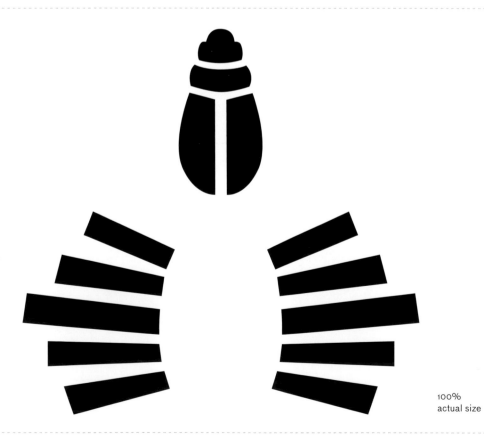

100%
actual size

## Block Out (page 52)

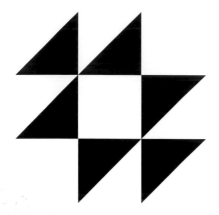

Enlarge
200%

## Junk Print (page 59)

Enlarge
150%

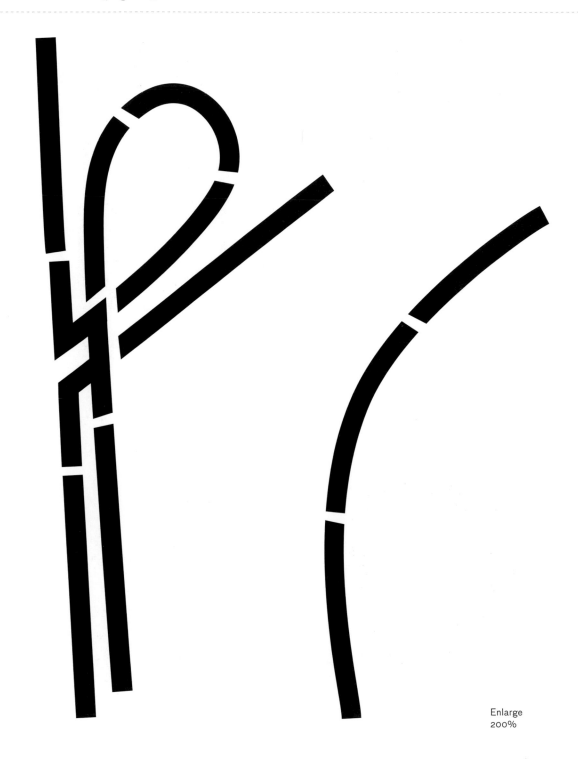

Enlarge
200%

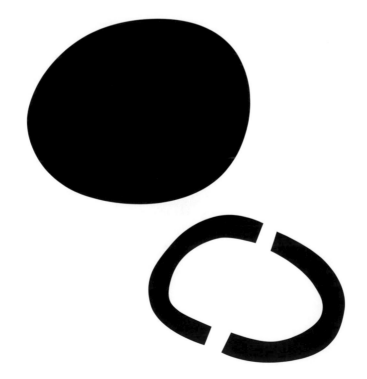

Enlarge
200%

Enlarge
150%

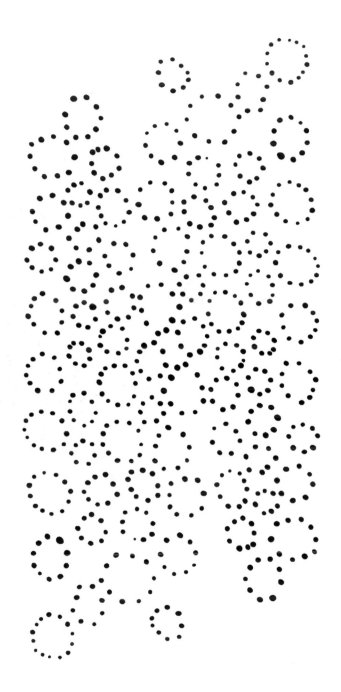

Enlarge
150%

Enlarge
150%

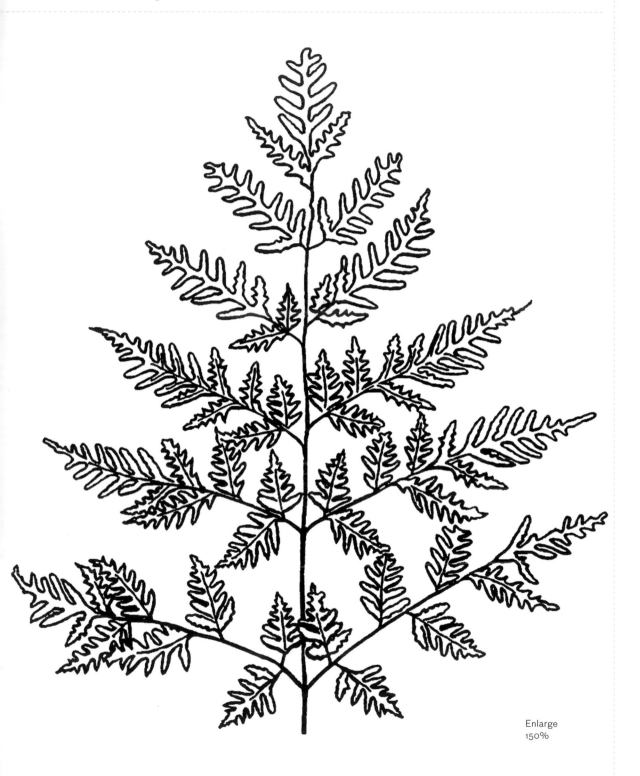

Enlarge
150%

**Sleek Sleeves** (page 113)

Enlarge
200%

Enlarge
200%

Enlarge
150%

Enlarge
200%

# Resources

## GENERAL ART SUPPLIES

**Pearl Paint**
www.pearlpaint.com

**Blick Art Materials**
www.dickblick.com

## OFFICE SUPPLIES

**Staples**
www.staples.com
*Iron-on transfer paper (I like Avery fabric transfers) and office supplies to repurpose for use in printing (e.g., numbers stamp and dot stickers with loose-leaf reinforcements).*

## FIBER ART SUPPLIES

**Dharma Trading Catalog**
www.dharmatrading.com

## FABRIC & TRIMMING SUPPLIES

**J. Caroline Creative**
www.jcarolinecreative.com
*Fabrics and notions.*

**M & J Trimming**
www.mjtrim.com
*Great NYC-based resource for ribbons and trims.*

**Yarn Tree**
www.yarntree.com
*Supplies for embroidery.*

**JoAnn Fabrics**
www.joann.com
*Fabrics for appliqué projects and embroidery supplies.*

**Michaels**
www.michaels.com
*General art-and-craft supplies.*

## SCREEN-PRINTING SUPPLIES

### Standard Screen Supply

www.standardscreen.com

*A major screen-printing resource, and a great place to have screens made from your artwork, using the photo-emulsion process. They can make film positives for you, too. Purchase screens, squeegees, ink, and other supplies. Information on making your own screens and other helpful tips are available on their website.*

### Valley Litho Supply

www.valleylitho.com

*Screen-printing supplies, including Union Aerotex ink (some of my favorite water-based screen-printing ink).*

## BLANK T-SHIRT SUPPLIES

### American Apparel

www.americanapparel.net

### Alternative Apparel

www.alternativeapparel.com

## FAVORITE T-SHIRT WEBSITES

### Threadless

www.threadless.com

*Submit your own tee designs!*

### Poketo

www.poketo.com

*T-shirts and other stuff designed by artists.*

## FAVORITE BOOKS

*NEOGEO: A New Edge to Abstraction* by Robert Klanten (editor), Sven Ehmann (editor), and Birgo Meyer (editor)
*Fantastic graphic inspiration.*

*Printing by Hand* by Lena Corwin
*A beautiful reference for fabric-printing techniques.*

*Stencil 101* by Ed Roth
*A great selection of stencils are in here.*

*Surface Design for Fabric* by Richard M. Proctor and Jennifer F. Lew
*An out-of-print book that has a really amazing selection of fabric-design techniques. It's worth hunting down a copy.*

## FAVORITE BLOGS

### Craft

blog.craftzine.com

*I miss the print magazine, but* Craft *online is great, too.*

### Design for Mankind

www.designformankind.com

### Earth Science Picture of the Day

epod.usra.edu/blog

*My absolute favorite!*

### Fly

Flygirls.typepad.com

### Oh Joy!

ohjoy.blogs.com

# Glossary

**acetate:** a clear, plastic sheet used for stencils and film positives. (Transparency film and vellum can also be used for film positives.)

**appliqué:** a decorative piece of fabric that is attached to a larger piece of fabric.

**backstitch:** a stitch sewn in reverse on a sewing machine to lock thread in place.

**brayer:** a rolling hand tool used for printing.

**color separation:** the process of making a different image for each color that you want to print.

**Diana camera:** a low-tech plastic camera that shoots 120 film. (I like it for the light leaks, soft focus, and unexpected results it produces.)

**drawing fluid:** a liquid applied to a silk screen to create an image. (It's used with screen filler).

**film positive:** a version of your artwork in black that is photocopied, drawn, or printed on acetate, transparency film, or vellum.

**flat side of silk screen:** the side of a silk screen that is flush with the edges of the frame.

**flat knit:** a fabric that is smooth.

**freezer paper:** a plastic-coated paper for kitchen and household uses that can be bought at the grocery store.

**French seam:** a seam that is sewn twice, on both sides of the fabric, to enclose raw edges.

**heat-set:** to heat your T-shirt to a very hot temperature in order to set the ink with a heavy-duty dryer or an iron. (A commercial dryer, like at a laundromat, works best.)

**iron-on transfer:** a sheet that can be fed through a printer to capture an image, then be transferred to fabric with an iron.

**linoleum block:** a piece of linoleum mounted on a block of wood that can be carved to use for printing.

**muslin:** an inexpensive, lightweight cotton fabric.

**negative space:** the area around the forms and lines in a piece of artwork.

## Glossary

newsprint: an inexpensive paper that is available at art supply stores. (I recommend using this for testing or putting inside tees while you are printing.)

opaque ink: ink that doesn't allow color to show through.

photo emulsion: a thick fluid used to coat a silk screen that allows a film-positive image to be transferred to the screen when exposed to light. (It's used with sensitizer.)

photoflood bulb: a light source used to expose a silk screen during the photo-emulsion process.

positive space: the forms or lines in a piece of artwork.

rib knit: a fabric that has vertical ridges.

scoop coater: a tool used to apply photo emulsion to a silk screen.

screen filler: a liquid that fills in the holes of a silk screen where drawing fluid has not been applied.

screen printing: the process of printing with a silk screen and ink.

sensitizer: a liquid mixed with photo emulsion to activate it.

serger: a sewing machine that sews overlock stitches.

silk screen: a screen made of mesh that is used in screen printing.

squeegee: a tool used to apply ink to a silk screen.

stabilizer: a thick, nonwoven fabric used as backing to secure embroidery stitching on knit fabric.

T-pins: long, T-shaped pins that are used to pin fabrics to a workspace.

tailor's chalk: a washable chalk used to mark fabrics when sewing.

transparent ink: ink that allows color to show through.

washfast: to make permanent through multiple washings.

well side of silk screen: the deep side of the silk screen with the raised frame.

# Index

# Index